Mark Zupo

Leadership:
From Ability to Credibility

Leadership

From Ability to Credibility!

By

Mark Zupo

Mark Zupo

Zupo, Mark

**Leadership
from Ability to Credibility!**

Copyright © 2009 Mark Zupo. Mark Zupo International, LLC All right reserved. No part of this book may be used or reproduced in any form without the prior written permission of the Author and Publisher. Printed in the United States of America.

ISBN-13: 978-0983994527
(Mark Zupo International, LLC)

ISBN-10: 0983994528

Library of Congress catalog Card #

Also available in Audio CD format

To order, contact:

www.MarkZupo.com

SlipperyRock Press™

DEDICATION

Dedicated to my wife,
Kay Stonesifer Zupo (1943-2005),
for saving my life.
Without whose memory, love, strength, support
and cheerful heart I would be lost forever.

In addition, to my Mother, Ann Rohrich, my
Daughter, Traci, brother and sister, Chris and Rene
for their undying support and love over the years.

I am forever grateful to you all.

Moreover, to my wife, Kathy, a tower of strength,
patience and support, who believed in me when
others failed me.

In your trust.

"The choice to lead is a choice to serve"
- Mark Zupo

Leadership:
From Ability to Credibility

Table of Contents

PART 1

1	How Does it Work?	9
2	Discovery	19
3	Self Confidence	34
4	Productivity Explosion	50
5	Communication Mastery	65
6	Mentorship Management	77
7	Strengths and Weaknesses	101
8	Attitude and Insight	114
9	Links to Self Insight	140
10	Observations and Growth	162
11	Learning Professionalism	174
12	Breakthroughs	194

PART 2   203

*Excerpt From the 2009 Interview and conversation with Speaker / Author and Thought-Leader Mark Zupo

Acknowledgments

Most importantly, the first person to thank is my Mother. Expressing my gratitude to her would take this entire book and encompass every emotion known to man, so I will just offer the most sincere thanks a son can offer:

"All that I am and all that I hope to be,
I owe to my mother."
-Abraham Lincoln

I would like to acknowledge those people who had and have a vision for finding their own success by helping other people find their success. I acknowledge those who have the desire to lead through service, sacrifice and accountability.

I also acknowledge those who selfishly seek and promote the desire to reward, celebrate and reinforce positive moral behavior and decision-making in all that we do in life through vision and values.

Leadership:
From Ability to Credibility

Chapter 1

How Does the Process of Leadership Work?

Here are the four key steps to building the kind of credibility and authority that commands attention from everyone within the sound of your voice or the reach your presence.

1. **Exploration and evaluations of goals and objectives**
2. **Foundation for laser-guided focus of your target intentions**
3. **Evaluation of your ambitions, purpose and aspirations**
4. **Execution of your action plan**

To begin, you must explore your intentions in a well-defined action plan in order to succeed in the manner you wish to succeed. Each action plan can be tailored to a specific project or goal and used to build relationships to the people who matter most. Once defined, you then create the informal and formal approach to achieve your goal for success. These are the time-tested principles of commanding leadership. The methods and system for positive influence, masterful communication, and definable trust to building unwavering loyalty are within reach for everyone.

Mark Zupo

Do you ever wonder what it takes to be an authority, a leader, a master at motivation, an inspiration to those that will listen to you? Well, here is the answer. You have the power to be all that and more. I have used the power of persuasion that is supported by years of command training as a Commercial Pilot and Flight Instructor to bring out the best in me. I teach simple techniques to drive people to self-awareness, self-worth, and self-confidence and ultimately to action.

A commanding presence as a leader and mentor are the foundation for absolute authority, credibility and success. In this book, you will:

- **Discover how to make an entrance that commands attention to YOU**
- **Learn how not to be taken advantage of because you're nice**
- **Find the secret to making people listen to you when you speak**
- **Capture the attention of a group in any topic of discussion**
- **Find out how to improve your self-image and self-worth**

For the last several decades, researchers conducted a hundred of studies proposing a number of characteristics that distinguished leaders from non-leaders: they include; intelligence, dominance, adaptability, persistence, integrity, socioeconomic status, and self-confidence just to name a few.

Leadership:
From Ability to Credibility

Read on to learn the profound rules for helping you to be recognized, to be admired, to be appreciated and to be an authority in your industry and personal life.

Your first lesson in personal success and commanding leadership is how to dispel the myths of Failure, Lack of Control, and Negative Influences of Other People. Find your "Real Dream System!" Your goals will empower you with the strength and desire to

"Don't just Be All You Can Be"...

"Be All You Want to be!"

If it has been done before, then YOU can do it, too! Be The First To Imagine It, and then...Achieve What You Can Believe!

There are two important differences between motivation and inspiration. They are some of the more insightful reasons for your success. Your homework is to understand why:

- **You are the Master of Your Success**
- **You are the Master of Your Achievements**
- **You are the Master of Wealth, Freedom and Happiness**

I believe that there are only three types of people.
1. The type of person that watches it happen
2. The type of person that makes it happen
3. The type of person who asks, "What happened?"

Which are you?

You can do three simple goal-setting methods before you are done brushing your teeth in the morning.

- Visualize your dreams to make them a reality.

- Affirm that you can do anything, be anything and achieve anything that anyone else can.

- Verbalize that you have to control your destiny or someone else will.

"Oh, really?" you ask.

"Yes really!" If it has been done before, someone just like you did it. So what makes you think that you cannot do it? They had money, they had time, they had help, and they had….who cares! You have the same resources, they are within reach, and…all you have to do is ask for it. Set a goal, make a plan and DO IT!

Leadership:
From Ability to Credibility

"You can't defend your excuses and then promote your successes"

- **Mark Zupo – 2009**

Leadership - It Is Everybody's Business

As a person develops personal skill and moral fiber, he/she should also develop professional character and proficiency as a leader. People are not born as leaders but acquire traits through experiences that may lead them to leadership roles whereby they are charged with the management and development of others. By definition, a leader is one who contributes to the team as much as he/she contributes to their reports. The level of stature as a leader is dependent upon the level of contribution that he/she makes to their subordinates and organization. Formal development as a leader is necessary to earn the respect of followers who trust in a leader's competency, character and effective decision-making abilities. This takes study, practice and engagement to be an effective leader only after an individual has mastered leading themselves. Self development is as crucial to success as can be gleaned from training, education and experience (Kouzes & Posner, 2007).

Mark Zupo

An effective leader practices the engagement, involvement, interaction and challenges to lead with character and with the opportunity to make a difference in the lives of those he/she leads. A leader becomes an effective leader through use of character-driven engagement, professional development training and support from experienced mentors (Bell & Smith, 2010). People willingly follow a leader who presents opportunity, provides vision and direction and integrates development and experience into their opportunity to grow and develop as individuals who are a part of a team. A key opportunity for a leader to grow is to learn as much about themselves as their followers. An effective leader is enabled to develop a plan for success, learn to use leadership skills and promote others to their highest performance while developing their skills.

The connection between a leader and his/her followers strengthens the connection between leader and follower and aligns the focus and intention of their combined efforts. The same traits that help an individual become a good leader in a responsible role are similar to the traits that help individuals develop into good employees (Kouzes & Posner, 2007). These traits aid in minimizing the gap between leadership and followers strengthening bonds and trust for a model, the inspiration of a shared vision, the challenge and enablement and encouragement that facilitates the dynamic processes between leaders and followers (Bell &

Leadership:
From Ability to Credibility

Smith, 2010).

The foundation for a base vision that is shared between leader and follower are the standards that set the course for ethical and decision-making in good judgment and to the benefit of everyone, not just the leader or organization. A culture of acceptance and encouragement is founded on a tangible opportunity to be lead by a set of rules. This measurement is the rule of standards that everyone is judged and measured similarly and equally. This opportunity presents a shared vision by standards that prevent a divided mission and sustain development and growth for everyone.

Encouragement is the substructure for personal development as individuals and followers who then will follow willingly and with enthusiasm. Mutual respect and recognition form a bond between leader and follower that is very hard to break once trust, confidence and reliance are entered into the leadership equation. Encouragement forms a motivational force that helps followers find their balance and value to an organization (Kouzes & Posner, 2007). The approach of encouragement aids individuals and leaders to feel the worth that is of personal value in a collective opportunity for growth.

Setting expectations develops a standard for performance that can be measured. A leader that sets expectation gives a follower the level of performance that is desired, milestones to gauge success and an expectation of a desired result. The result is the value that is represented by the follower once any level of achievement is realized (Bell & Smith, 2010). To answer in the affirmative when these expectations are met presents a follower with the motivation and inspiration to expend greater effort to achieve goals and expectations because the reward is equally as valued. The result for the follower and for leadership is predictable performance to grow and expand on.

Recognition and reward are fundamental to development and satisfaction in work and play. Recognition is a tribute to performance and accomplishment by followers and the organization. Reward develops pride in one's work and respect for leadership's ability to drive the mission and vision for the benefit of everyone involved. Reward develops a culture of celebration for success no matter the level of achievement (Bell & Smith, 2010).

An important aspect of trust and collective mission and vision is building community among members of followers and between leadership and members. The accomplishments of everyone in the

Leadership:
From Ability to Credibility

organization provide the community of the organization to collectively bask in the rewards of the community effort. Cultural transformations take place when the organization realizes that they are a community who must trust and rely on each other for success and development (Deal & Peterson, 2009, p. 11). This condition is the need for achievement that drives the personal desires, the need for affiliation that drives the social desire and the need for power that drives the collective engagement of all members as an entity (Bell & Smith, 2010).

Leadership by example challenges the notion that leadership only benefits the leader and not the follower. Leadership by example is defined by the leader's ability to create a vision based on one's own vision, sets strategies for successful engagements based on one's own character and ethical performance, communicates a clear goal that benefits everyone and empowers followers to their success beyond personal gain and individual benefit (Northouse, 2007). He influence of leadership by example develops trust and loyalty that is historically exampled in military exercises between leaders and their subordinates.

Learned Leadership is formed from self-development as a master of individual skills and character. Learned leadership is a lesson in self-development and mastery of self. Learned leadership contains convictions of wisdom and values within one's soul that are formed from experiences and education (Kouzes & Posner, 2007). The ability to make improvements in moral management and balancing human potential with responsibility and initiative forms a point of reference for leaders (Wasylyshn, Shorey, & Chaffin, 2012) formed point of reference sets the direction for leaders as their guide for development and maturity. The result of a mature leader is one that provides for their followers as they expect to be provided for. The balance of earned leadership traits from experience and education will produce the contributions to organizations and individuals.

Leadership:
From Ability to Credibility

CHAPTER 2

Discovery

"Who you are perceived to be tomorrow is what you were believed to be today"

- **Mark Zupo**

When my wife, Kay, was diagnosed with Cancer, we immediately sought the finest care that money and insurance could buy. Her cancer was called, Pseudomyxoma Peritonea, a horrible form of internal Cancer associated with the ovaries and appendix. Kay was given 3-months to live. At the time, it was incurable, un-treatable and usually fatal. Little did I know what the real cost of this disease would be. It was not just the implications of surgery, travel, medical expense, fear and illness. It was the absolute evacuation of everything we knew as normal.

We could not understand or pronounce most of the medical terms we had just learned and our medical bills started to grow immediately. Kay's disease would be the catalyst for many far-reaching events from that moment on. First was the travel to find any physician that knew anything at all about the illness. That was a daunting task.

We traveled to the Mayo Clinic in Jacksonville, Florida, and sought care there from a physician we thought knew something about it, Only later to find out he really did not. We discovered he relied on our ignorance to give her basic care and an initial operation that was to help some, but not address the problem. That was $280,000 later.

The insurance company, here un-named to keep from suing me again, refused to pay for that foray because the Cancer operation the doctor performed was considered experimental. No kidding. Experimental...and it did not qualify for benefits. They refused to pay for the operation expenses so I had to and I did. Two-hundred and eighty-thousand dollars out of pocket. I was fortunate to have it, or so I thought.

Kay survived the operation and was to see a few extra months of life at a somewhat normal existence. We relied on the doctors to know the answers and thought we had made the right decision based on that. We would be wrong.

Kay had a second operation that failed to fix anything. She died within thirty days of coming out of the hospital. The total cost to me, aside from her life, would be well over $1-million 400,000 dollars. I would lose my job within a

Leadership:
From Ability to Credibility

month of Kay dying. I would lose my credit within a month of that. I would lose my home within 3 months to foreclosure. Five months after foreclosure came bankruptcy. In one years' time, I lost my wife, my job, my savings, my home, my credit and my dog. Yes, my beloved 13-year old dog passed too.

There was no federal help for me, no consideration because everyone else was out of a job, no unemployment because I was self-employed, no bailout because I was a small business owner, no extensions, no lawsuits...nothing. Flat dead broke and alone and no one could give a crap. All this at the doorstep to the current financial crisis. I relied on the system to keep me when I was down and it failed me. I paid into the system for over 35 years in every way, shape, and form and I got nothing.

My reward for years of taxes, on-time payments, support for my community, paying for the finest insurance, being an up-standing citizen was zip, zero, nada and "Go away because you're untrustworthy, a credit risk and worthless." Considering the definition of reliance again, reliance is a certainty...reliance is the certainty that if you rely on anyone other than yourself you will lose. "They" will take everything you own in a flash and make you feel like a fool for trying.

How do you combat this? What does this have to do with leadership? Why must I be a leader just to get along in life?

Leadership sets you apart from the crowd and enables you to divisively attack life's challenges with resolve and determination. It is up to you and only you. You must learn everything about what protects you and yours, from those you will rely on. You must learn to be self-sufficient and independent. You must learn to inspect what you expect. Trust comes from knowledge. Empower yourself by educating yourself with the tools to make your own way. Use your experiences to be certain. That is reliance.

Many studies have been done and many books and articles have been published on this subject of leadership. What has emerged are a consistent set of leadership attributes. An effective leader does most, if not all, of the following:

- **Challenge the Process**—search out challenging opportunities, take risks, and learn from mistakes.
- **Inspire others to come together and agree on a future direction or goal**— create a shared vision by thinking about the future,

Leadership:
From Ability to Credibility

having a strong positive vision, and encouraging others to participate.
- **Help others to act**—help others to work together, to cooperate and collaborate by developing shared goals and building trust, and help to make others stronger by encouraging them to develop their skills and talents.
- **Set an example**—behave in ways that are consistent with professed values and help others to achieve small gains that keep them motivated, especially when a goal will not be achieved quickly.
- **Encourage others**—recognize each individual's contributions to the success of a project.

Another way of defining leadership is to acknowledge what people value in individuals that are recognized as leaders. Most people can think of individuals they consider being leaders. Research conducted in the 1980s by James Kouzes and Barry Posner found that a majority of people admire, and willingly follow, people who are honest, forward-looking, inspiring, and competent

An individual who would like to develop leadership skills can profit from the knowledge that leadership is *not* just a set of exceptional skills and attributes possessed by only a few very special people. Rather, leadership is a process and a set of skills that can be learned. There are approaches that we can take to get around each corner in life when we face adversity and challenges that are presented when we grow and help others to grow. A leader is someone who typically does not wait for things to happen but makes things happen. Instead of waiting for things to happen, self-insight prepares us for what is coming.

The challenge for leaders falls to three pillars of empowerment that I call the Three "Sights."

Insight

Foresight

Far-sight

Here I explain the semantics of the three "sight" support system.

Insight

Self-insight is guided by our natural instincts, which helps us to see consequences of our actions before we commit to them and act on them. Thus, one builds other skills while developing self-insight, such as the ability to stay focused. In addition, one improves his or her ability to make better decisions with self-insight. The skill provides you the ability to work through professional growth, which is the way to improve your leadership skills. Self-insight is a learned trait and is fostered by our need to improve progress and develop.

Leadership:
From Ability to Credibility

You can decide on what course to take before you jump into any situation that requires the traits of a leader. For example, if you see that you need to take a course of action to improve your skills before applying for a better job, thus purpose will move you to action.

It is crucial that we better our skills in order to survive the advanced technology changes taking place each day. The advancement of technology is so strong that it requires many skills for us to make sufficient income to survive. For example, as soon as a new computer hits the market, and when someone buys that computer, taking it out the door, the PC is already outdated based on the technical requirements of the business world and academic advancements already in progress. A new one is in the making long before that computer goes out the door.

Foresight

For this reason, you need to learn how to use self-insight to make good choices that helps one through professional growth. Otherwise, when the future continues into higher-grade and more advanced technology, you might be one of those sitting on the waiting line of unemployment. Life requires that we continue learning. Learning continuously will help one stay well versed in today's high-dollar technology sectors. Therefore, it is essential that we all turn inward to see what it necessary for us to advance toward the new age world. Learning is the key to leadership abilities.

"Learn - to - Earn"

Turning inward is a process that takes time, preparation, practice, mediation and meditation. Time is essentially valuable to us all. We want to learn how to use our time wisely by cutting back some of the things that only hold us back from finishing other duties or self-imposed assertions. Therefore, it is wise to start working toward professional growth by setting up a time management plan. The plan will give you the insight and knowledge that you can use to make progress. Prepare, since it will help you stay focused, organized and set up an effective time management scheme.

When it comes to trying to find the answers internally, you have to dig deep into your soul and your mind to find the right answers that suit your

Leadership:
From Ability to Credibility

needs and wants as well as those that apply to your socio-economic and cultural demands.

It is a long process and no one will tell you that it is easy, yet you can accomplish much by putting forth effort. So let me tell you how you might to learn how to get started. You have to be able to take a long look inside yourself sometimes, this is not easy for anyone but in order to be able to find answers it has to be done.

Searching your mind and insight will help you to find your hopes and dreams as well as to feel motivated enough to make your wishes come true. This is all about finding yourself and makes you have a better insight of your self-worth and value that you present or represent to another person or employer.

Sometimes it takes some time to become a professional but as you grow, you will find that it will be easier for you to handle your responsibilities. This will help you to be able to define who you are and what you want in life as an individual. This may help you to become a successful businessperson. In order to become a professional you have to work at it. This is not going to be something that does not take any time or effort; this is going to be an ongoing duty.

Mastery of your field and endeavors establishes who you are by definition as well as by profession.

Mark Zupo

Sometimes people will experience hard times but you will have to learn how to overcome this and walk through it. You will not only cross over the divergence but you will come across many self-emotions and experience the power of self-growth. You may feel anxiety, fear, resentment, guilt and a lot of uneasiness. However, when you are feeling this way all you have to do is to learn to overcome it and move forward, you do not want to go backwards that would be defeating the whole purpose of what you are trying to accomplish.

How does one get on the right path? It will all depend on you and your frame of mind and how fast you will progress. It is going to take some time but as you learn to work on it, it will come to you faster than someone who only thinks they want it. This is going to take some time you will have to work at this every day until you get what you want or in until you are happy where you stand.

Perseverance, dedication, persistence, resolve and tenacity are the rule of the day

NEVER QUIT!

Leadership:
From Ability to Credibility

However, you will find out you will also have to work at this all the time. In order to become that successful person that you want to be, there is work that you are going to have to do.

Some of the things that you may have to do to get where you want to be by sitting down and creating some goals. It does not matter how long they are or how short they may be. Once they are down on paper, then you are going to have to learn to work at achieving your goals. You could even hang them in the kitchen since everyone goes to the icebox for something. This way you can see them and read them each day to keep your mind fresh. When you recently read something, it will soon sink in and this will make it so that you will always be working on your goals. Once you have your goals you will see that the rest will come naturally.

We can make breakthroughs by looking inward at our own abilities. Self-insight is a working skill that helps us to develop new skills. We can look at our experiences, past, and knowledge to make our life better.

Visualize Your Success

Confidence and Confluence!

Mark Zupo

Far-sight

By probing, in the self, one can exploit the search into the mind and make new breakthroughs, develop new ideas, and find solutions that will direct you on the way to professional growth. We all need to expand our skills.

From the time that we are born, we often think, or at least we wonder, what is our fate? We often think that this is the journey that lets us drift into the streams that confuses one. Many people stay insides these areas.

Why should you have to stay in a confined room when you are able to get out and see the world? You will then be able to notice that the world can offer you more than you think it can. If you are willing, it can offer you the biggest pot of gold that you will not even be able to use both hands to move it. Inside this pot of gold there is a river flowing deep with the knowledge of processional growth.

The inside of our self-realization has all the answers we will need to be able to find that path the will lead us to find that professional growth that we are all looking for in life. All you will have to do is take a little trip inside that mind of yours and you will be able to find that inner self that you have been searching for. This will really amaze you and give you the information that will channel you and help you to reprogram your ways of thinking. This will send you on your way to the path of

Leadership:
From Ability to Credibility

professional growth.

Once you have tapped in to all that you and have used up all of your fuel you will have to find another source to get fuel you tank filled back up to be able to move to the next day. We have to sometimes get into the source we do this by using meditation, self-emending or even when we go exploring. There are so many ways that you are able to get into your insights and be able to use then to help you to get to your professional growth. You as a person have to be willing to get there. This is going to take some time but can be done.

These will be some of best techniques that you will be able to see evidence of when put into action. You will want to set your goals so they will meet your purpose in life. This will give you something to look forward to and be able to keep you motivated enough to be able to reach your goals.

These goals should be set so that you are able to reach the businessperson in you. Some people will be able to do this and then again, there are some that will have to strive to reach what they want in life, this will also affect that professional growth line that they may want to use.

When you want to become a professional, your state of mind is the crucial link to success. If you want to see, what professionalism is then you are going to have to discover and meet the standards, skills, and the character that is expected by highly trained people that work in this field every day. Inspiration and Energy

> *"Success is an Inside Job...In Your Heart, In Your Mind, And In Your Spirit. Only you can bring it out"*
>
> **- Mark Zupo**

Once you have decided what you want in life and your career direction, you are going to want to make sure to keep your plan of action fresh and top of mind. Therefore, am going to tell you a few things that might help you to do that. Achieving a professional status is a daunting task that requires education, practice and devotion to that goal.

Many things are available to you that you can do to help you to keep your professional status alive. What you have to do is research so it can help you to learn more as well as to keep up with all the new technology that is coming out every day. It does not matter if you are a mail carrier or a daycare provider, a homemaker or astronaut; there are always new ways that are there to try to make your success improved for you.

How do go about learning how to keep up with technology. There are always classes that you can take to keep your mind fresh of all new things

Leadership:
From Ability to Credibility

that they are coming out with. Sometimes you may have to take a major class to keep up with all the support that you need to be able to carry this out.

You have weakness; then again, we have strengths as well. Using your weakness to define your strengths is a valuable measurement tool for success.

It is hard to be able to keep your strengths viable if you do not do something about it. You have to be able to learn all you can even when you are feeling like there is no hope, because there is always hope. Do not give up keep going until you are unable to go any more. Roadblocks are simply hurdles that test our willingness to charge forward. So keep your head up and go as far as you can to make your success a reality.

Your strength is the tool for achievement.

"You have to look up to get up,

You have to get up to move up,

You have to move up to be at the top"

If there is a way, then find it, never quit and always move forward. One-step in front of the other. Sometimes it is into uncharted territory but forward nevertheless.

CHAPTER 3

Self Confidence

**"Passion delivers purpose,
Action delivers results!"
Make your business...your business!**

- Mark Zupo 2008

A good leader provides for the vision and mission that his followers will direct their energies. Each action that a leader takes will be perceived by his peers and organization as the character of his organization. It is crucial that a good leader serve all people as well as his organization selflessly and with great character and moral disposition. Respect is the key factor when considering a leader's ability to lead with clear direction a concise focus. To do so, you are challenged to lead from a position of ethics, moral standard, mission and a sense of direction and vision.

Have you ever taken a long looked in the mirror to see the real you? We all have at one time or another, while looking at yourself your looking within yourself this could be you trying to find answer to a problem that you have been able to find the answers to or maybe you just want to be able to find who you want to be. Are you looking in the mirror to see who you are or to see what you

Leadership:
From Ability to Credibility

are to other people? Sometimes self-examination is a healthy thing that might reveal a weakness that requires your attention or a focus boost to your self-confidence. We must all dig deep within our self in order to find answers that help us to improve our quality of life.

For some of us that want to make something more of our life's there are some things that we have to do, in order to be able to find our self. We have to be able to understand what we are thinking as well as feeling. Here are three main ways that we find who and what we are.

The first thing is self-examination. This is a process of self-initializing your dreams and desires. Once you figured out how to self-examine yourself then you can move to the other areas like meditation. This will make it easier to be able to think more clearly as well as be able determine your identity and value.

You will also have to have good self-esteem in order to learn.

Becoming a professional is one thing but to be able to use it wisely in the work environment is another thing. Mastery of your skills is crucial to your success and self worth as well as to those that are in your professional environment. Right alone with the other entire task you are going to learn. Find your way to self-growth.

Mark Zupo

C.H.A.R.A.C.T.E.R.

Each of the letters in the word CHARACTER stand for an ideal that drives home a crucial and applicable point that character is the foundation for all that you are and everything you are perceived to be. Each letter sheds light on an example of the definition of character and what it has meant to me and what it can mean to you and your success.

Commitment

Commitment means to show loyalty or duty to someone or something. It should be the pledge or promise to you for personal growth. Most importantly, your commitment should be to live a fruitful and productive life by living your dreams. I wanted to be an astronaut and then I actually applied? Well, I did not have the "right stuff" but I sure had the dream and never stopped believing that I could achieve it! Never.

Help

I became a boy scout and respectfully learned the meaning of help. It was not until my good friend, Carlos, lost his son in a freak accident that I learned what help meant. A week before his son went to Puerto Rico to visit relatives; Carlos and I picked up his son, Michael, up and took him for an airplane ride. He was a great kid. A bit quiet, but a great kid who was thrilled to fly with his Dad. A week later, his father would be flying to him to try

Leadership:
From Ability to Credibility

to save his life.

Carlos's son, Michael, went with his mother to Puerto Rico to visit relatives over the Christmas holiday. While there, Michael fell from a chair in a freak accident and hit his head. He suffered a concussion, which resulted in a brain hemorrhage that ultimately cost him his life a few days later. Carlos, a flight instructor like me, made little money and could not afford the airline ticket money to go to Puerto Rico to be with his son.

What you might be thinking is that I gave him the money. Carlos asked, but I was broke as well and did not give him the money from any resource that I had. I tried to raise the airfare but came up short. A decision that I would come to regret. He eventually found the means and traveled to bury his son. I would have thought that this incident would have driven our friendship apart but rather, it made our friendship stronger. I am not sure why it happened that way...but I am never the less, grateful.

Our friendship grew as strong as any brothers did. Maybe better. We were truly best friends, comrades and fellow pilots. I discovered after Carlos's own death that I helped him in another way. I was the support for him in understanding Michael's death because I had lost my son as well. That is when I learned that help and support comes in many shapes. It is not always about money. Help when you can, where you can and because you can, but not because you have to. This is character.

Allegiance

Allegiance is an obligation of devotion and or loyalty. Loyalty is the most valuable of all traits that anyone can deliver to their friends and devotion is the most honored of all traits that empowers those around you. When I was despondent at the loss of my son, I committed acts that would undermine my credibility as a father, husband and business leader. I held no allegiances to anyone for anything because I withdrew from society, from my marriage and my life's work. I became the "island" that we hear about in novels. It is a very lonely place. I fear, yet today, that I crossed someone's path or touched someone's life when in my deepest rage that was more hurtful than helpful. I fear this because I firmly believe that you can touch a person's life with the simplest gestures that can alter their future or change their destiny in a way less valuable than would have been. This is a huge responsibility.

The saddest part of this time for me was that I all but ignored my wife's grief and despair at the loss of her son as well. I would regret this, too. One day when I was at my lowest, Kay told me that she loved me no matter what I did or did not do. She asked me not to leave her until I was thinking more

Leadership:
From Ability to Credibility

clearly. Kay also gave me the one thing that remained in my life that meant more than any money or success, my daughter, Traci. Traci reminded me that I was still her father and she would never understand my plight or my devotion to her just because I lost a son.

On the day, we told Traci that her brother was killed and would not be coming home she only said one thing, "I don't want to be alone." It was on that day that I learned what devotion and loyalty meant. As a young child, she understood more than we thought. She understood that because we were grieving that we would retreat from her. That is what she meant about "being alone". That my friend is powerful stuff. This is character.

Results

A result is the final consequence of a sequence of actions or events. The possible results include advantage, disadvantage, gain, loss, value and victory. There are possible outcomes associated with an event depending on the point of view, historical distance or relevance. Reaching no result can mean that actions are inefficient, ineffective, meaningless or flawed. This is important.

It was not until I collected my thoughts after losing my son, that I realized I had given away almost a million dollars, most everything I owned and some of my credibility and respect. The results were devastating to my ability to think clearly and function normally. I have come to learn recently of the long-term effects of being an idiot and arrogant person when I ran into a former business associate who refused to do business with me because of who I was back then. When he realized that I was a different person, he mellowed and was accepting. We have since completed many deals and have profited from every one. Remember to consider the results.

Affirmation

Affirmation is a declaration that something is true. When I was a young boy living on the farm and at the dump, I learned the value of what is true and what is not. My stepfather was not a bad man, just a gross example of the inability to raise a child, manage a household or keep a family. His methods of discipline were tantamount to brutal interrogation, delivering physical submission and berating one into compliance. The one thing that struck a chord with me was when he continually called me, "a dummy". That was even more effective than the repeated verbal abuse or threats of physical violence against me or my mother.

A child can deal with being hit because the pain goes away in a while. However, being berated and mentally abused remains for a lifetime as long as memory lasts. I suggest that any person one-hundred years old cannot remember being paddled

Leadership:
From Ability to Credibility

but everyone will remember being told they were too stupid to learn. How that is associated with affirmation is that you have to believe it for it to make a difference. I firmly believe that I found it impossible to get a degree and complete college because I inwardly believed that I was too dumb to learn. After all, my father said so, is that not right? Wrong! For whatever reason I failed, it was because I somehow compensated for being stupid because I was told I was stupid. It was affirmed that I was stupid because an adult said so and it must be true. Wrong again!

One teacher, with whom I studied at the age of forty-four, told me that I was one of the smartest people she had ever met. She was amazed that I had achieved so much, millionaire status without a degree, on my own out of sheer determination just to prove that I could do it. Just to prove that I was not a dummy. I built three businesses and was a huge success because I needed to affirm that I was good enough.

So what then was holding me back after that? Nothing! Because a teacher affirmed that I was more-than capable of attaining a degree, I did it. In fact, I did it three times!

I returned to college at 44, attained a Bachelor's degree, continued to a Master's degree, a second master has and attained several PhD-level certifications, certificates and awards for my efforts. I am not a dummy and will never be poor again. As long as I can learn, I can earn. This is the stuff of character.

Conviction

A conviction is a compelling admission of truth and or a strong persuasion of belief. I knew in my heart that I was a good man. I was just as good a man now when I was poor as when I had money. It is often said that money makes either a good man better or a bad man worse. I do not necessarily believe that completely because there are many people with a lot of money who do leaps of good for humanity. What I have always found interesting is a person who will donate millions to charity just to relieve him or her of a tax burden for being so rich. That is not conviction. Their motive is not an example of what conviction is defined as.

Conviction is what supports the truth about who you are and what others think you are. When I was richer I made it a goal to help other people at my expense purely to help and not because I could

Leadership:
From Ability to Credibility

gain something from it. I have lent money without expectation of repayment, even when offered. I have donated when the need was there without giving my name. I have offered help in the simplest and the grandest form and never asked for recognition. I am not a philanthropist and barely a humanitarian. I am convinced that you must earn your keep and earn the trust of those with whom you associate. However, when a person is down on their luck and in need, you help them whether you need to or not. That is conviction.

Trust

Trust is the reliance on another person or entity. Having faith in others and believing them. This is a biggie with me. Trust is an absolute necessity in every part of your life. The lack of trust has caused wars, famine, disease, destruction, economic failure, global unrest and a list of adjectives too many to mention. Trust is the foundation for every success story ever told from the Bible to present day politics.

In the process of flight training, an individual must study, train and be examined just like in any school setting, except with airplanes. When I was training to get a Commercial Pilot's Certificate, I worked feverishly to learn every procedure, tactic, method and skill that I would need to pass the test and actual flight exam in a twin-engine airplane. My

Mark Zupo

FAA Pilot examiner, Mr. Mike Sheldon, was a military experienced and now civilian flight examiner based in Alabama at the Madison County Executive airport. Mr. Sheldon was chosen to be my examiner to determine my status to become a commercial pilot.

With some fear and trepidation, I flew my twin-engine aircraft to the Madison County airport to be examined by Mike Sheldon. After meeting him, I sat in his comfortable but modest office surrounded by memorabilia of his achievements. It was a bit overwhelming and exciting at the same time. I could not help but think that there was not anything I could or could not do that would escape a man with thousands of flight hours in hundreds of aircraft among dozens of war-experienced pilots.

Without going into detail, I passed the verbal exam but failed the flight exam. It was the first aviation exam I ever failed. It seems as though someone forgot to put the landing gear down prior to landing. No, we did not crash, because Mr. Sheldon took action and redirected the flight back to a safe altitude. I felt as though the weight of the world was on my shoulders because I made the most serious of errors, I was about to cause a life-threatening accident when no such condition existed for it to happen on its own. Mr. Sheldon made me feel as though we had crashed the effort to drive home the point of my responsibility under every condition and to reinforce my attention to

Leadership:
From Ability to Credibility

details if I was to ever be a Captain. It became eerily silent in the cockpit as we went around for another attempt knowing that I failed the final test of my ability as a pilot in command miserably. After all, even if the flight goes well it does not bode well after a safe flight to kill all the passengers upon landing at their destination!

Believing I would never fly again and upon exiting the plane, Mr. Sheldon said, "Prepare yourself for another flight and we'll do it again." To my disbelief, he was going to give me a second chance to kill him...or so it seemed. We boarded the aircraft and took off. I was sweating like a hog in the summer to think that I might make another mistake and end my aviation career in Madison County, Alabama. With that in mind, he gently said that I should go through the procedures and land the proper way this time. Well, that I did. I went around the pattern like a professional pilot with exacting skill and touched down...gear first of course. I was elated to realize I had passed. Mike then said, "Let's go around again."

Mark Zupo

I thought, "Oh NO, what did I do wrong? It was a perfect landing." Truth be known, I did it perfectly and Mr. Shelton was about to rebuild my trust. When approaching the airfield he asked me to put on goggles that obscured my vision; the kind of goggles we used with night training making it impossible to see out of the windshield. Therefore, I did and then he told me to land the plane...blind! I said, "Excuse me?" He said that he would visually guide me to the runway and verbally direct me to the proper attitude, direction, altitude, decent rate while I controlled the yoke and landed the plane!

Leadership:
From Ability to Credibility

He said, "Trust me, you can do it and I stake my life on it." I thought he must have a death wish, was crazy or something but I listened and obeyed his command. In the last minutes of our approach, I used every instrument and skill I had ever learned directing my aircraft to as picture perfect and smooth a landing as had ever been made. You read right, I landed a plane blind, no visual, just instruments without ever seeing the runway, the ground or the airport. I am living proof that it can be done because I did it and lived to tell about it. I did it because Mike Sheldon knew I could do it. He trusted me and told me so. That, my friends, is trust.

Excellence

Excellence is the state or quality of excelling. In business and organizations, excellence is considered to be an important value, and a goal to be pursued.

The quality of your life is directly proportional to the effort you demonstrate while striving for excellence. I once heard a statement about reaching for the moon when trying to achieve a goal. Les Brown said, "If you reach for the moon and fail, you are still among the stars." I do not think there is a more true statement for realizing success. Let me explain.

I dreamt of becoming an astronaut as a young

boy. I thought I could achieve that goal just because it wanted very badly. I had no idea I could not do it. I had no idea I was not capable of reaching that goal. I did not know I was not smart enough to realize that dream. To me, there were no barriers.

Reliance

Reliance is a certainty based on your experiences. I will define good reliance and bad reliance. The reason for both is detailed in experiences that will hurt you or will help you. Let us talk about the bad stuff first.

When I was just starting out in life as an entrepreneur I relied on other people's expertise to guide me to good decisions...the decisions that protected my family and my money. What I got, instead, were the decisions that benefitted my advisors more than they benefitted me. By the time I started my first entrepreneurial venture and saving money, I asked a friend in my church where I should put the money I was making so it would be protected and make me more money. He advised me to put it into an annuity. Not good.

An annuity for a young person was the worst idea that has ever been invented, unless you are the advisor! You see, the investment counselor made huge sums in fees and commissions from my money and all I got were losses and taxes. Eventually I lost over $80,000 dollars because I

Leadership:
From Ability to Credibility

relied on someone else to guide me when I refused to learn the basics myself. Who is to blame? Me. The lesson that I learned was never to completely rely on anyone else for anything that I could not learn about myself. Now, let us talk about the good reliance.

Remember that I described the definition of reliance as a "certainty" based on personal experience. After 30 years of saving every penny that I could, building my "empire", developing relationships, nurturing friendships and business associations, paying every bill in full and on time, owing no-one and making my way as a leader, entrepreneur and respected member of my community...I lost it all in less than 2 years.

> ***"The will to win, the desire to succeed, the urge to reach your full potential... these are the keys that will unlock the door to personal excellence."***
>
> **Confucius**

Chapter 4

Productivity Explosion

> *"You can't have a testimony...
> until you've had a test"*
>
> - **Unknown**

We all face many challenges daily, which make it difficult for anyone to stay focused, positive, and to worry about develop professional growth. We all face the various economic problems, such as unemployment and poverty. Despite that these issues exist, we still must stay focused however. Many people are discouraged from the leaders and government who are stealing their freedom each day.

This is leading to the declining in morality and familial values. Many people fear the potential risks of warfare and terrorism attacks. Other issues include homelessness, corruption, aggression, declines in ethical and principles, as well as fairness is affecting our life and economy each day. Economic issues, such as gun and gun control, as well as energy crisis also affect our lives.

These factors have a devastating effect on our productivity **because they divert our attention and focus from our intention and direction.**

Leadership:
From Ability to Credibility

We see a need to make changes. We all must look in the mirror, looking deep within to see what changes we need to make. We can only change ourselves, so it is important to focus on you when you work toward professional growth. Socialism, such as cultural strife reached to 8% and 14% throughout the years, very little modification are made that give good reason because of the inclining toll of problems we all face today.

Racial discrimination is one of the foremost issues that we all must sort out and we are influenced by this in our workplace, schools, and other areas around the world.

Human behaviors are the way one behaves; this is reflected on our self-image and on our relationship with others. Psychology spectators define behavior as the way one behaves or responds to specific set of conditions. Along these lines, we see that influences tap into how one reacts. For this reason, we must focus on the development of social skills while observing, and maintaining a healthy influential life while associating with other people. We need positive people in our life to make it to professional and productive growth.

Mark Zupo

The psychodynamics interplay with our mental responses. It determines the way we think, feel, or wish for something. It connects us with the mind or way of thinking that we establish. It directs us to see that behaviors take place from mental proceedings. External regions of our consciousness also tap into this proceeding and our mental processes often will conflict with one another, especially if we do not take the time to reprogram the mind to abandon misconceptions. To become a professional thinker, one must leave behind childish thinking, or feelings, such as bias, stereotyped ways or thoughts, and so on.

Do not continue being part of life's problems; rather become parts of a solution that will make your life more fulfilling. Professionalism will drive you down the long-winding road to success. Your productivity will suffer and your ability to affect others productivity will suffer as well.

Learning is a part of life. This part of life will help you to abandon or leave behind any misconceptions that get in the way of your progress. Continue to educate yourself in productive habits by reading articles and other information to find ways to enhance your productive professionalism.

Leadership:
From Ability to Credibility

Here are five ways to increase your productivity.

- **Track It -** Keep a daily log of your activities for two weeks then determine which things are essential and which things are not. If the task does not contribute to your overall goals, you may want to consider eliminating it completely.

- **Prioritize -** Break your essential tasks into three categories; Urgent, Vital, and Important. Perform your open tasks according to how important they are to increasing your personal productivity while making choices on how to use your available time.

- **Delegate -** Ask yourself if someone else could do the tasks for you. If so, outsource the work to a peer or subordinate. Even if it only frees up 30 minutes, that is 30 minutes more that you can use to complete some other tasks.

- **Stop Making New Commitments -** If you are having trouble keeping the commitments you have already made, stop making new ones until you are caught up. It isn't against the rules to say, "NO".

- **Relax and Enjoy Life** – When you are trying to increase your personal productivity in order to accomplish something you should divide the *time doing real work from the time you are at work.* What is it that you are trying to do - Have more family time? Make more money? Whatever it is, you need to remember to stop and have fun along in the process. Life is a journey to a destination as well as a process to live better.

Commanding Presence

You know a person when you see them enter a room by their commanding presence. The one everyone notices because they are a natural leader. It may be their body language or their attention to detail with the masterful return look from them. How do they do it? There are people that are subconsciously recognized for their leadership abilities from the first opportunity for advancement. What is it that they have that you do not?

Our cultures are quite socially advanced but we still remain held to some primal instinct of position and power. A confidence and status based upon many things said and unsaid. It seems that presence commands the confidence of anyone around them. It is a sort of energy that is automatically recognized for the power that it reflects. There are three key factors that affect our command of presence:

1. **Posture**
2. **Eye contact**
3. **Body Movement**

These factors are crucial in commanding the room among peers, subordinates and authorities

Leadership:
From Ability to Credibility

outranking you. They are the primary factors in initiating change in your favor.

When you want to be able to make changes, you have to be able to a have a positive attitude. A positive attitude will help you when you feel worn out from making all the necessary changes to improve your professional growth. When one has a negative attitude then they will have a bad attitude toward life and everything around them. Therefore, we have to learn to get rid of the negative thinking so that we can have a positive attitude toward life as well as be able to make our self-feel better so that we can make a better life for us and the people that we love.

Posture -

A speaker never leans backward when presenting. A successful and commanding speaker always leans slightly forward toward their audience. A confident posture is always the best practice for a successful position in the hierarchy.

Do you realize that your physiological performance has a reflection on the mental and emotional attitude? With this attitude, it will help to develop how well you see things that reflect on the way you feel about things in your life. We deliberately use our critical and the thinking abilities that can and will reflect our ways of actions as well as the accomplishment and the way that we succeed in life.

Mark Zupo

We have to learn to get off the couch stop being those nice little couch potatoes, when someone is lazy it will or could affect the way they think as well as have a reflection on our actions and make it hard to be able to be successful in the world today. Our attitude is mostly developed by how you see things. If we learn how to take actions on how to have a positive attitude, it might lead us to become successful in one's life. For this reason, we need to cultivate a positive attitude and maintain our position.

Here are some negative reflections that we may want to look at. These will help us to figure out what we have to do for our self in order to get successful. Some of the things that we need to look for would be confusion, agitation, feebleness, senile, overwhelming stress, victim of the bad and easy prey. Here are some of the positive reflections would be accomplishment, active, regal, accepted, leadership, motivated as well as energized and being in control. This will help you to become successful in your life as well as to learn how to get in control of your actions.

The way you feel and your look play a big part on your success in life and in your profession growth. How are we going to learn how to deal with this what can I do to make it happen? The first thing you have to do is to go deep inside yourself and decided why and how to change.

Leadership:
From Ability to Credibility

Eye Contact -

Your attitude is reflected in your eyes. They are the window to your should and it is your soul that should shine through when presenting yourself for approval from your peers, subordinates and superiors. People search for your motives in your voice and it is best reflected in your eyes. Direct eye contact is a direct link to your ability to tell the truth. The truth in turn is reflected in your attitude first.

Your attitude is something is carried with you throughout your life and is reflected on you and everyone around you so you should think about this if this is a problem for you. Your attitude will go everywhere that you go; it is as if your shadow so if you think you may have a problem with this then you may want to try to do something about it as soon as you are able to do it. Your attitude will go with you with your work as well as your life style. The way you are thinking reflects on others could put a dent in your professional life. Trust and authority go hand in hand with presence. Violate one of them and you undermine your presence.

When trying to change your attitude you have to work at it. It will take some time, but can be done. With some time and a little studying, you will soon see a change your behavior. Times are hard as you already know this and with you having an attitude, it is just going to be that much harder on you. Therefore, if you are able to do something about it you should. Having a good attitude will help you to have a better outlook on life in general.

When wanting to know if you have a positive outlook on things you need to be able to scale your feelings as well as your emotions, right along with your thoughts. This will make you be able to see things with a different eye. There is evidence out there that will help you to see that when one improves there psychological and physiological states that they will feel a lot better and command a better presence in the company of others. The higher state of mind that you may have will help you to improve your health as well. When you are feeling better about you it will lower your risks of heart disease, the stress levels in your mind and body, as well help you with your immune system this will help to decrease the risk of an early demise.

Body Movement -

Body movement should not be confused with posture. Your body movement is a direct reflection of your thoughts. Think that someone else is a mind reader when they ask, "What's wrong?" What goes on in your head is another direct reflection of what you display when you present to those around you. The working nation of employers substantiates this in their hiring practices. There is support for this theory in the support for the younger, less experienced candidate than for the older perspective employee due in part

Leadership:
From Ability to Credibility

because of their ability to present themselves as youthful and vibrant. This then becomes evident in your attitude.

There is a lot of reason to try to change your attitude on life for it will be easier for you to success in life with what you want as well be healthy for you when it comes to your health. Finding the way to living healthier is a type of insurance that you will make it through professional growth. Despite the pressure to perform or the hardship that you might face, present yourself immediately as confident, sure and certain by presenting a positive motion in your body movement.

Take some time to search the Internet to find ways to use insight to manipulate through the physical growth phase to arrive at the door of professionalism and presence. You will improve your life, make more money and welcome positive friends into your life. Filling your world with positive influences makes it easier to carry the load or weight that life puts on your shoulders. Online you will find a wealth of the latest information that guides you in the right path to professional growth.

Look for the updated articles and read some of the older news to find techniques that help you make the most of professional growth. The information flowing online includes self-development, which are the steps toward professionalism. Be sure to read how others have worked through self-development to build their skills and qualities. Build your willpower as well, so that you can flow inside self-insight to professional growth. Remember, leadership is not always about power and power is not always about leadership. Each compliments the other when they are held together by your presence.

Goals, Strategies and Values

We can evaluate the natural environment viewpoint of behaviors, as well as the ways it affects our life every day. In keeping with the nature of sciences, this is one of *the largest part of dramatic* manipulate influences that have an effect on our mental process. For the reason, the point of view established by primitive philosophers lead behaviorists to analyze the issues further and then to was to reconcile the argument by questioning the area under discussion more systematically and methodically.

To give a broad, balanced coverage of all-important areas in your life, try to set goals in some of these categories (or in categories of your own, where these are important to you):

- **Career:**
  What level do you want to reach in your career? Who do you want to be?

Leadership:
From Ability to Credibility

- **Financial:**
  How much do you want to earn and by when?

- **Education:**
  What information and skills will you need to achieve other goals? If you can learn then you can earn.

- **Family:**
  Family is the most important aspect of life. Loneliness claims more success than any other condition.

- **Attitude:**
  What part of your mindset holding you back? Is there any part of the way that you behave that upsets you? If so, set a goal to improve your behavior or find a solution to the problem.

- **Physical:**
  Good health ensures lasting and vibrant ability. What steps are you going to take to achieve good physical health?

- **Pleasure:**
  Your life belongs to you, own it to enjoy it.

Delving into the sciences of behavior, behaviorists employed a collection of approaches, which commence with using appropriate course of action of "conducting psychological research" that cool, calm and collectedly went into a "meticulous concentration of the systematic" line of attack, which became the forerunner that guided them to look at carefully scientific structures and the experiments.

Scientists have used many techniques to analyze behaviorism. This is due to the many problems that people have with developing professionally through self-insight. One of the tests was the diametrically scientific observation of a rat. This rat was encouraged to run through a mesh, or maze. During the test, the suckling was attached to a synthetic nipple. This was to help him make a "movable turn" during the test. The results showed that the heart rate inclined during the sound of a signal, or bell. It was noted however that before the test started that the suckling was given electric shocks.

Many experts thereafter claimed that none of us has the capability to observe direct cataleptic purpose or motive. Because of the results many scientists and behaviorists paved the way to developing other scientific applications. The standardized applications are regulated and enables scientist to compare similar behaviors through observational learning.

Some believe that these predictable test results can be used as an example to help people work toward professional growth by using self-insight. Evolutionist use some of the same applications, which has become one of the most

Leadership:
From Ability to Credibility

essential solutions that has helped scientists find reason to justify the facts revealed. The applications used over the years to explore human behaviors have directed many others to study the chief sub-disciplinary structures in the psychology, as well as in the workplace. These biopsychology studies reach into human behaviors and mental processes in order to help experts and others to examine the physical foundations, which cause stress that develops from thoughts and targets the emotions.

In the social channels of psychology, as well as in the clinical and cognitive, the focus here channels into professional growth and into the work fields. This is the I/O or the industrial and organizational sectors, as well as the health, educational, and other applications that are applied in the studies to help scientists and others to understand human behaviors.

In today's business world requirements are setup in various companies putting more emphasis on the need to develop professional skills and qualities. Essentially, more and more companies are putting up higher demands in order to create a harmonized and structured environment. For this reason, many people are considering continuous education in order to continue learning and meet the requirements imparted to them by various organizations around the globe.

Mark Zupo

Japan is one of the major areas in the world that expects professional attitudes in the work field. China and Tokyo is another area that has a high demand placed on professional growth. This pattern is spreading, which in time, every corner of the world will require that people focus on using self-insight for professional growth. What are the ratifications? Use this acronym tool for remembering your goal setting method. The "SMART" method of goal setting:

- **S** Specific
- **M** Measurable
- **A** Attainable
- **R** Relevant
- **T** Time-bound

Hold yourself accountable for your successes and failures.

Leadership:
From Ability to Credibility

CHAPTER 5

Communication Mastery

When it comes to self-development and understanding others, it is almost like a seemingly endless rollercoaster ride that never seems to stop. Just when you think you have figured out someone, new development stages unfold and you are back to learning again. When you work through professional growth by using self-insight, it pays to keep the golden rule in sight. "Just when you think you know it all, you soon find out that you know nothing at all." This is a never-ending cycle for all of us.

To understand others as well as the self, you must go through this permanent episode of changes and development. By the time you become a young one in the infancy phase, you already have a measure of achievements. This is part of the recognition of interacting sociably, which takes you to a mutual stand in growth. During this stage, infants tend to develop this view that their other individual dealings are based on the self.

We analyze perceptions. We carry on finding out how they play into using self-insight for professional growth, which also takes us around the circles of theorization that develops in the mind. Throughout adolescent and beyond we move into the "perspective-taking" phases, which drives us straight into the gutters of understanding one's ability to view others and the way they may see things.

We use visualization tactics to examine others and the self. Using these same tactics one can expand his or her professional growth through inner insight. Using visualization combined with affirmations we can clear any doubts from our minds. This includes self-defeating doubt, such as doubting one's ability to reach goals. We all have this ability. Some are sluggish, some of us miss the points, and some other of us makes it to the finish line. You want to be one of those on that finish line by develop professional skills.

You can make it to the finish line through training, practice, exertion, and using techniques that work for us. One of the best ways to get started is by assessing and measuring your weaknesses and strengths. You will also need to recognize how these strengths could be chink in somebody's armor, and how your weaknesses could be strengths. By recognizing these elements of your strengths and weaknesses, you can move to take action. This action will involve the improvement of your skills and abilities.

We are often preconditioned by influences surrounding our environment. Very few of us are mavericks, which are the nonconformists. These are the free spirited souls. Preconditions are a focus here in the "perspective-taking" development phase. This falls alone the theorization and

Leadership:
From Ability to Credibility

unconditional ideas in regards to beliefs, thoughts, self, feelings, others, psychological states, and one's own continuation.

To develop businesslike skills and qualities one must learn to conform to standards of skills, competence, and characters that are commonly expected in a work environment. In order to move in this direction one must advance in the development phases.

Many people struggle to recognize the differences amid reality and unreality. This is because the use visualization as a form to produce fantasy-fiction thoughts, rather than non-fictional dreams. This is one of the predecessors that stand in the way of many people's success. One must learn to visualize self while staying in the real world and accepting that the world is both good and bad.

Theorization plays into perspectives. By applying theorization rules one can understand, listen better, and perform mental and physical activities whereas that entity is consciously aware of his or her behaviors. We can use our observation skills to advance any skill we possess.

Powerful Leadership Skills

At the bottom of emotional starting place over and over again causes people to produce constructive or unenthusiastic thoughts. Over the course of one's life, they must take the road to unconscious, conscious, and subconscious learning to figure it all out. In the mind, we have channels that enable us to improve our professional, personal, performance, and other skills. We have the root of knowledge from our learning, experiences and events that we can draw from to advance toward professional growth.

One's way of thinking when optimistic can help that one to institute self-belief, which allows this one to build on the confidence through practice. Constructive social communication and self-help methods can help one to establish a new way of thinking.

Our discernment and commencement reflect on the self and others. Often we must reprogram the mind to reframe our way of thinking. It is up to each of us to take action to adapt our way of thinking. The world is a big place and offers many rewards, so why not step into self-insight, and advance toward professional growth. This is the start of building confidence and self-esteem.

We all have propensity and parallel individuality. Each of us seeks appreciation, admiration, love, and other constructive enforcer to make one stronger. We all must feel engrossed in something and fit into place. The common denominators say to us that all of us have the ability to use self-insight to advance toward professional growth. We all need encouraging influences in order to make it over the hurdle of

Leadership:
From Ability to Credibility

self-development. The problem however is that many individuals panic at the thought of change.

Change however is something that helps us to grow. Change is advancement and gives us prospective ways to improve our skills and abilities. Change enables one to adapt and make de rigueur or obligatory adjustments.

We need to develop an understanding in order to keep a clear mind. We need this clear mind to decide how we should respond or react to any situation, be part of the cause, verbalize, or generate a working natural environment. Change drives one to acknowledgment. This makes the entity feel the need to be in the right place, feel a sense of acknowledgment, and so on. Revolutionize changes can help build self-confidence and inspiration. All of us must institute a self-reliance to develop self-confidence. By paving the passageway to your advancement, you will exert the self-harder, working on the way to building self-confidence and a winning way of thinking. We must pay attention to constructive feedback, since it helps us to adapt to making changes that drive us to professional growth alley.

We need to put emphasis on our progress while seeing things in a broad spectrum. By checking one's internal and external advancements and growth, one can recognize his abilities and give rewards for the progress you have completed. We must stay focused. Focusing on one's competency and professional skills will help you to keep growing. We must fundamentally thrive to focus on the positive, and let the negative go. We can place great emphasis on accomplishment, motivation, management, performance, and other skills. We are obligated to recognize that our constructiveness is the way to encourage the self by reflecting on one's introspective, self-evaluation and correction progress.

To learn more about developing a positive attitude for self-insight and professional growth, visit the Internet today. You will find loads of valuable information posted online. Look along the new age arena to find the latest techniques that have been helping people through professional growth for years. Start the decoding process today.

Building Authority

"As an authority, you have to earn the right to get paid.

In a doctor's office, you might drop your shorts....
In a dentist office...you don't!"

- **Mark Zupo 2009**

Leadership:
From Ability to Credibility

All of us have the power to make changes in the way we think, feel, or conduct our self. We can consider our level of development, knowledge, experiences, and the proceedings from the precedent years. We must practice natural techniques, which can help us to stay focused. Once preparation starts, we must weigh the difference amid unconstructive and positive. Rumination is the processes of thinking deeply on a subject. This course of action moves one through the process of discovery and developing original ideas.

Human expansion experts often have the same opinion that if one focuses on developing healthy self-esteem and virtuous quantity of self-belief that entity can prevail over the unhelpful acts, feelings, behaviors, and so forth. A measure of the solution involves the interaction with encouraging influences. These influences will help you find a way to perceive things differently and often will activate your spirits with a few friendly words that come from well-rounded knowledge, contented moods, pleasant appearance, trustworthiness, and so forth.

How one contributes to information in some measure influence what mind-set we develop. Being around negative people all the time will only hold you back from professional growth. When you step into this growth arena, you want to arm yourself with the best breastplate that life can provide. This will ensure that you meet the expectations all the way through this growth phase. You must remove any negativity in your life to advance toward professional growth. Below is a list of negative that you can work on: Be sure to take action as soon as possible so that you become the pro that you long to be.

- **Racism** – the variants of racism only lead you to intolerance and bigotry. Do not be listed in this category, otherwise, you will not succeed in the business world.

- **Hate** – if you are filled with hate, revulsions, you are someone disgusting to others. Abandon hate and people will like you.

- **Dishonesty** – if you are dishonest, people will not trust you. Mendacious people often commit fraud or other crimes, simply because they set themselves up for the fall.

- **Disloyalty** – disloyal people are unfaithful, false, or fake, treacherous, and untrustworthy. Do not be a fictional character in someone's book rather develop faithful traits.

- **Doubt** – When you have doubts, you will often hesitate when it is your turn to make a decision. If you are indecisive, people will consider you mistrusting, will feel suspicious of you, skeptic to listen, reserved, and so on. Do not be a smidgen. Rather become a lifelong learner, and adjust your way of thinking by finding the facts.

Leadership:
From Ability to Credibility

There are many other negative thinking habits you should consider. You should also consider your behaviors and habits. If you have unconstructive habits or behaviors, they often lead you straight down the road to damnation. You want to avoid hitting this road, since no benefits are offered. The only true outcome is self-defeat, self-destruction, and self-annihilation. Understand that you can extract from negative to produce positive.

By developing a winning sense of humor, you will start to see things in many ways, rather in a negative way. Learn to laugh and be cheerful. Everyone enjoys a person full of life. Imagine yourself sitting in a big, overstuffed leather office chair with a big fat expensive cigar in your hand. Often the relaxed people make it to the higher office grounds. You can change in many ways, but try to keep it on a real note and on a constructive level so that you can improve your overall quality of life. Dismiss those negative thought.

MASTERING CREDIBILITY

*"**The right attitude gets the right results**"*

- **Mark Zupo - 2010**

Maslow made some great points when he commented on the "hierarchy of needs." As stated by his viewpoint led him to believe that needs follow a formation, which all plays into professional growth. This structure involved a "lower level needs" that started with the fundamental continued existence that must be satisfied "before higher level needs guide a person's behavior." One of the highest levels is the need for "self-actualization."

After a short time ago, I began my journey writing about self-actualization, which is the flourishing personal development that necessitate for one to employ personal skills and abilities to attain and maintain professional attitudes.

In the workplace, many people have higher levels of needs that commence with basic survival skills. Other people are on the lower need scale. The ones on this scale tend to have inner guides that direct them toward professional growth. We see that the individuals that have higher needs are channeled down the right course while the lower level needs are not.

With this in mind, we can see that someone could without problems form predisposed opinions of another, and make obvious their stereotype behaviors that interject a work environment. To some of us, labeling or categorizing others is one of the largest problems we all have to deal with, and shape the way one thinks, which is brought out in the open in their behaviors each day.

An additional drawback in the workplace is pointed out in various periodicals that speak of favoritism. Preferential treatment in the work

Leadership:
From Ability to Credibility

environment has repeatedly caused many issues that decline the count of professionalism. Employers and employees have a duty to show fairness to one another. Each of us has the responsibility to treat each other equal. This is an EEOC fair opportunity act in progress. The many consequences one will face for not illustrating EEOC characteristics and by ignoring the policies and procedures, thus the consequences should be the same for all.

Bosses must treat employees equal; otherwise, it could cause conflict in the work environment. People often develop hostile attitudes when they are not treated justly. With so much competition in the world, as well as the low morale issues, lack of respect, etc., it is hard on all of us, which is why equal fairness should be demonstrated each day.

We all must develop professional behaviors, thinking, and so on to rebuild skills that were torn away by the entire negative that takes place in our world. We must reform our thinking and behaviors while staying clear of negative people.

Despite that, these rules exists many employees, employers, and even the law ignores these rules. Mary also tells us "In the work environment, the supervisor, owners, or managers are responsible for motivation. The morale on the job will determine the success, attitude, and dedication of the employees.

Being positive, honest, and treating employees with respect will create a positive work environment with working and willing employees. Introducing new ideas, teamwork including supervisors participating, rewards, understanding personal, and business issues will motivate staff to meet deadlines, be attendance conscious, and adhere to policies and procedures. A motivating supervisor with a positive attitude will gain the respect of the employees and the willingness for their contribution to be complete and concise."

You can find more information online. It only takes a few minutes to check out the Internet to find additional information to help you grow. Go Internet today!

Leadership:
From Ability to Credibility

CHAPTER 6

Mentorship Management

"Build your strengths by nailing down your weaknesses"

- **Mark Zupo – 2009**

A level of competency is necessary to enforce that one succeeds. Competency is built on experience and knowledge. By gathering information, you can build on knowledge by finding the facts. Gathering information will, in time build skill, realization, and wisdom.

Professionalism is becoming one of the major requirements for employees and employers in the business world. Because of the many problems, businesses are placing greater emphasis on education and learning. Some of the changes in business have led to major changes and expectations. Businesses are supposed to be a place where people exchange ideas without conflicts. Many of the conflicts that take place in the businesses and real world are due to lack of professionalism.

The world is moving rapidly toward Internet business whereas many companies are selling products, services, and so forth online. E-mails are being sent each day, which has posed issues. Many businesses are expecting employees to write professional electronic mails to promote their services or products. The problem with this is that the employee must learn proper marketing strategies, writing, and other skilled tasks to ensure that the connections are meet without complications.

Internet providers will bar those that send emails in spam form, so company employees must learn to prevent, act, and respond to emails without violating the Internet providers' rules and policies. Therefore, new training is underway and employees and employers are encouraged to advance their professional growth by using their self-insight. Other issues are present that is causing a crisis, which is inspiring businesses to encourage employees and employers to adapt to professional attitudes.

Leadership Development

The Paths to Self-insight and Professional Growth

Self-insight provides us imminent approaches that we can take to get around each corner in life. Instead of waiting for things to happen, self-insight prepares us for what is coming. Self-insight is guided by our natural instincts, which helps us to see consequences of our actions ahead of time.

Leadership:
From Ability to Credibility

Thus, one builds other skills while developing self-insight, such as the ability to stay focused. In addition, one improves his or her ability to prepare and make better decisions with self-insight. The skill provides you the ability to work through professional growth, which is the way to improve your job skills.

Insightfully, one can decide on what course to take before he or she jumps into any situation. For example, if you see that you need to take courses to improve your skills before applying for a better job, thus self-insight will move you to action.

We all must better our skills in order to survive the advanced technology changes taking place each day. The advancement of technology is so strong that it requires many skills for one to make sufficient income to survive these days. For instance, as soon as a new computer hits the market, and when someone buys that computer, taking it out the door, thus that PC is already outdated. A new one is in the making long before that computer goes out the door.

For this reason, many businesses around the world are encouraging employees to develop technology skills. Most companies these days require that you have at most minimal skills in technology and some basic knowledge of computers. Those that do not have these skills often fall in the cracks on the lower employment scale.

For this reason, one needs to learn how to use self-insight to make good choices that helps one through professional growth. Otherwise, when the future continues into higher-grade technology, you might be one of those sitting on the waiting line of unemployment.

Life requires that we continue learning. Learning continuously will help one stay well versed in today's high-dollar technology sectors. Therefore, it is essential that we all turn inward to see what it necessary for us to advance toward the new age world.

Self-Insight and Professional Growth

Turning inward is a process that takes time, preparation, practice and meditation. Time is essentially valuable to us all. We want to learn how to use our time wisely by cutting back some of the things that only hold us back from finishing other duties. Therefore, it is wise to start working toward professional growth by setting up a time management plan. The plan will give you insight and knowledge that you can use to make progress. Prepare, since it will help you stay focused, organized and set up an effective time management scheme.

Leadership:
From Ability to Credibility

How to set up a time management plan: First, think about your daily duties. Think about what you do when you finish your tasks. Next, think about what you do when you are not managing your projects. How do you spend your time? How much of your time is spent handling a single task? How much time do you have in a day? How much time do you spend sleeping? How much time to you spend on entertainment? What about activities or family time and how much time to do you spend mingling with friends.

Once you have finished answering each question, sit down and reflect on your answers. Make sure that you write them down where you can review your notes later. Once you have finished reflecting on your answers, take some time to go over your notes.

Now, make a list of your things to do. Write down the time you spend on each task. Record the time you spend outside of work with family, friends and entertainment. Continue until you have calculated how much time in 24 hours each day is spent on a single action.

Use your list. You want to cut back on time, so make sure that you mark on your list the most important project you must complete each day. How much time can you save by managing one project at a given time? How can you clear up time by preparing for the project ahead of time? Continue, until you have a well-written list of, to do tasks, which are most important. Each day take care of your most important duties first. Prepare before you start. Keep your desk clear of clutter so that you are sufficient prepared to finish your major task in a timely manner. Have your accessories, such as pens, paper, paperclips and other items handy. This will cutback some time, since you will not be looking around for them. After you finish your major task, start working through your list until you complete each task.

Monitor your time spent per task without allowing it to interfere with your responsibilities. Use a timer. With each task finished, record the time you spent working on the task. At the end of each day take some time to see if you managed the project in a timely way, or if you could find other ways to cut back on time by finishing the task sooner. Stay focused while you work through the time manage setup scheme. Take each step slowly, yet progressively so that you are effectively capable of cutting back time.

Next, move to your home. What do you do once you arrive home? Do you spend hours watching television? Do you spend time with family and friends while putting off other responsibilities? Try this...when you come home, do your chores first. Get the household responsibilities taking care of and then spend some time with your family. Have a nice family dinner with each of you seated around the table. Spend time communication. Find out how

Leadership:
From Ability to Credibility

each family members day went.

Once you are finished, you may want to relax. Spend an hour watching television with your family and then get your "next day," clothing and ideas prepared. Take the set of clothes you intend to wear the following day out of your closet and sit them somewhere where you can get to them quickly in the morning. Continue preparing until you have at least 30 minutes each moment to spare of relaxation.

Professional Growth and Self-Insight

Time –

Money –

Preparation –

Practice -

Skills and Techniques -

365 days each year, many people spend most of their time running around and making sure, they did not leave anything out. Throughout their busy schedule, they spend much of their time consumed in thinking about what they are going to do after work.

Now, statistically speaking, if 3000 people, 365 days each week spent 8 hours in a day worrying about what they would do after they get off work would be around -16,653.125 guesstimated wasted time spent on nothing they have no control over at the time, and each day. Since we have over 5.5 billion people in the world, this figure quadruples. It may serve as no significance, however, with every second burnt in each day, and is another dollar spent. This is part of the reason why our economic prices rise and fall each day. Now you know why people use the metaphor, time wasted is money burned.

Over half of the time wasted could be spent on professional growth and the development of self-insight. If even half of the 3000 people spent more time focusing on their jobs, rather than what they will do after work, it would also cut back on time that could be used to do something that is positive or constructive.

This moves us to see the importance of preparing. Preparation helps us to save time and money by allowing us to stay focused on what we need to accomplish. Let us see how it can save us time by preparing and focusing on what we need to do. Take the same example above. Per se, 3000 people each day head off to work and during work, their main focus is centered on what they need to finish first. The estimated amount of time saved each day - 16,653.125 plus 16,653.125 = 333, 062.5 and you would calculate half this figure, multiplying it because additional time would be

Leadership:
From Ability to Credibility

saved by the 3000 people completing their tasks in a timely manner. Thus, time is added to this picture and money is saved. This would equal about 66 million minutes of time saved in each year. Wow!

Now, if you prepared you could add some more time saved on to this figure, which means that your boss would love you and you would likely get a raise and promotion. During the time you save, you can invest some of the added time into developing your self-insight and professional growth.

Since each of us is different, it is up to you to figure out how you can swing it. Some of us for example, can think about self-development while manipulating through tasks effectively and staying focused. Of course, this is a psychoanalytic mental thinker type, but it is possible to train a normal person to work through self-development while working and focusing on his or her tasks.

How is this possible?

First, understand that a psychoanalytic mind will walk through a series of self-development procedures at the same time that person is evaluating the patient through advanced observation skills. This means you would have to develop your self-insight, awareness and build on your magnitude of conscious awareness. You would likely need some subliminal learning training if you are one of the average thinkers in the world. Practice then is the one of the essential keys to progressing in self-insight and professional growth.

Through practice, you can improve your motor skills, and other skills. You need sufficient techniques however, that work for you. Practice is no good if you do not have something to practice with. For this reason, you may want to visit the Internet to get in on the latest techniques for self;-development.

Discoveries in Professional Growth

We make discoveries when we look into our own insight. Our insight streams from our events in precedent times, and form from our experiences and knowledge that we retained over the years. By analyzing, the self one can tap into this mind and make new discoveries, develop ideas, and come up with solutions that direct them toward professional growth. We all need to improve our skills. This is a given.

From the time of our birth, we often wander through the development phases drifting in an out on and off. It seems to become an aimless journey that drifts us into the stream of confusion. Many people stay within these boundaries. Instead of being stuck all your life in a nuts' shell, climb out and see what the world has to offer you. The world can offer you a pot of gold, but it takes you to reach out and take hold of the pot in order to start digging deep into the realm of professional growth.

Leadership:
From Ability to Credibility

Our inner self has all the answers we need to find the pathway to professional growth. If you are willing to take the adventure inside the mind to find this inner self, you will find amazing information that will channel you, reprogram you, and send you on your way to professional growth. Tapping into your own fluids will give you the fuel you need to fill up your gas tank and move toward a better tomorrow. We often tap into this source by meditating, self-examining, or self-exploring. There are many other ways that you can also dip into your insights and use them to work toward professional growth.

For now, these are some of the great techniques. You want to set goals so that you have a purpose. Purpose will give you something to look forward to and will keep you motivated to continue reaching your goals. Business people come in all forms. Some business people are well rounded, while others are like you, striving to reach the professional growth line. Some other business people fall in the cracks while others continue reaching for the top.

Professionalism to an extent is a state of mind. Professionalism is the form of meeting standards by applying skills, competence, and character as expected by members of highly trained experts. A professional looks at attire despite that they have their own style. For instance, if a professional comes from the Western atmosphere and accustom to dress in this way, thus the professional will make adjustments despite it is not right to accommodate a northern style. Professionals are often stripped down of their self and put into a position that accommodates others.

Sometimes you have to give up likes to adapt to the professional world. In the end however it will pay off, simply put because someone bigger than humans are standing up for your well-being and will stand behind who you are. The sacrifices are deep, but the rewards are great.

The professional is someone assertive. This is a fight in its self. Why, because everyone you know will call you every name in the world, but someone that is trying to do what is right. You have defense however.

Look within. I cannot tell you how many people I stand to each day that seems to think that they have all the answers and I am an unfair person. Let me tell you, it is not easy telling someone NO….simply because they see this as something negative. This is a completely new level we must discuss, but the problem exists. If you are going on the professional world, step into reality, because people will bite you every step of the way.

Weak Self-Insight and Professional Growth

You can build on your insight, which in turn can help you advance to professional growth. One of the best ways to build on insight is through

Leadership:
From Ability to Credibility

continuous learning. Lifelong learners often advance to higher planes of consciousness, which leads them to the development of professional manners and attitude. Lifelong learners build confidence, self-esteem, and often see things in broader views. It becomes a habit that they continue to use throughout their lifetime.

Professionalism is often judged by one's appearance as well. However, some people have such a high professional attitude that no matter how they appear in the public eye, people recognize them as professionals. Professionalism means more than making more money. It is about self-growth, which an entity will build on his or her qualities and skills, as well as reform the way of thinking and behaving.

Librarianship is one of the conditioned people geared up for success. Often these people continue learning by studying, reading, and referencing. Each day the librarian collects information, organizes the text, preserves the books, and continue to supply access to the public to gain knowledge and information. This is one of the most fulfilling missions. Librarians will preserve important records of culture, which is handed down to proceeding generations. Libraries offer a stream of communication by passing along history, future, and present knowledge and information. Librarians often govern, learn, play, and work on a balanced structure.

Mark Zupo

We can learn from the librarian by building some of these qualities. Possessing these skills and qualities will inspire professional growth on a balanced scale. Experience and success go hand in hand. Thus, advance your experience and you will find yourself wearing a professional attitude. Keep in mind that professional growth is a lifetime commitment. Once you get started, you must not let up until the end of your days. Professionals often volunteer their time as a service of goodwill to others. When you volunteer your time, you feel good inside about you. The action will inspire you to continue your journey in life through the process of professional growth.

Professional growth functions on competence, communication, and ethnical understandings. This is a well-rounded entity that has abandoned negative thinking, actions, and behaviors. Some of the characters stripped from this person are prejudice, hate, envy, strife, grief, sorrow, and so on. Another cornerstone of professional growth is integrity. Professional people uphold honesty and truthfulness. They are reliable and upright with everything they do in the public eye. Some people believe that professionalism is extremely overrated. To some extent it is. This is because all people see professionalism in a different way. Some people may think of professional people as snobs. The fact is professional growth is necessary if you want to survive in this world.

Leadership:
From Ability to Credibility

Professional growth builds dignity. Dignified people have a nice poise, self-esteem, self-respect, and stand out from others. A true professional is noble and impressive. Professionals often develop good social skills because they realize the importance of communicating and intermingling with other people. This characteristic helps them to get along well with co-workers, bosses, or anyone in their life.

The professional person is confident in public because he or she had adapted their viewpoints in accord to standards. Still, professional growth is about more than having professional manners. Professionalism is a component that includes character and principles. Professional growth spawns various thoughts. Building on our self-insight for professional growth leads you to success. Despite what you may think, professionalism is a component fit for everyone. It is the only way that we can make it in today's world. Insight can help you program the mind to think and act professional.

Insight Programmed in Professional Self-Growth

An abstracted value does not solely describe professional growth. It is a fundamental element we must develop to perform safe operations in civilized environments. One's professionalism – is the specialized standards that create skill, competence, and temperament that is anticipated of any person of a highly trained organization, and it changes with each individual. Some people have a higher grade of specialized manners, while others are still at work developing these qualities and skills. Professional growth helps us to build multi-leveled skills. It is a fundamental element in any professional field. In some business sectors, professionalism is a prerequisite and any individual must have a superior grade of competency. This is the foundation of social communication.

New York Raised the Bar on organized professionalism reclaiming it as "energy affordability." Its variants are camaraderie of purpose, which is inexhaustible. Professionalism paves the way to essentialism to create a rock solid institution. Professionalism is more than the clothes you wear; it is the central part of contact entrées. It is a self-growth plan and a service. The paramount traits are esteemed in many areas of the world.

In Japan, Tokyo, and other native lands, professional growth is necessary in order to transmit messages via Pros. Attitudes and skilled levels create a professional person. Some people believe that professionalism is more than the way one behaves or appears to the public eye.

According to some spectators, professional growth is never enough, nor is it the good of the adversary of the noble! Uncompromising professional growth is also implicated in a readiness to try. That is why professional growth is not

Leadership:
From Ability to Credibility

actually an ism. Opposing to this predominant idea or understanding, assessment of professionalism is deficient. In educational sectors, professional growth is crucial issues that need reformed.

We must work toward developing professional qualities and skills by learning. Professionalism is how one does business, and with superiority is how one handles any services. It is crucial to announce that professional growth is important. It is also appropriate. Professional growth is the client of assisting services. Professional growth is the foundation of aquatic knowledge amid society and communication. Various qualities validate professionalism, but taken as a whole, professionalism is both an attitude and a standard of living for the workplace.

Professional growth combines attitude with style. In European countries, it is the keystone and the path to success. Human resources professionalism is one of the fundamental components of a superiority initial care or school-age curriculum.

To make it in this world we must use self-insight to work toward professional growth, which is a lifelong commitment. Ceasing growth is not an option. While all people view professional growth in many ways, the primary focus is noted in the trail of occupations whereas people are expected to act businesslike. They must conform to the standards of expected skills, competency, and character. This person must show a high level of skill and competency. It is a habitual action that usually becomes annoying for many because they indulge in a specific activity often.

Still, it is a requirement. Self-insight is the way one perceives his or her personality. Using this tool one can change the way he or she sees the self, and reflect on seeing the self as someone in the professional world. Insight is our perceptiveness, which makes up our ability to see clearly and intuitively into the nature of complexity, other people, situations, or subjects. Using this self-insight you '6can objectively see your way to professional growth. To learn more about using self-insight for professional growth visit the Internet to find articles and more. Develop your skills.

Skills in Self-Insight and Professional Growth;

By no means is professional growth centered on just skills alone. One must expand his or her knowledge and experiences as well. One of the better ways to do this is through continuous learning. Remember, just when you thought you knew everything, you find out later that you knew nothing at all.

Developing a professional attitude, way of thinking, and set of behaviors is important in the business world today. Many companies are now making this a requirement. In fact, AOA, ACGME, adopted the minimal program GCs that states that

Leadership:
From Ability to Credibility

professionalism is one of the six practical competencies. Professionalism is the opponent to pretext. Understanding, experience and professional growth is a promise of success. Professionalism however is more than success and making money. It is a way of life we all must adapt to in order to survive. Develop expert skills and qualities will increase energy flow so that you can focus on success.

In a broad-spectrum, professional growth is exemplified by unity of reason. Foremost, the call for professional growth is boundless. Professional growth and self-insight is not a conclusion in itself; it liberates fundamental keys. One can build a rock solid platform by expanding his or her professional growth through self-insight. Besides clothing, professional growth is the foundation of success.

Various descriptions and decisive factor for professional growth have been projected; with the majority of theorists either signifying that professional development is not a succeeding or failing event entirely. Professional growth is a self-improvement plan and a service. Some spectators, such as SYSTEN believes that professional growth is dominant. Others think of professional growth as valued.

Professional growth is as much or more than an attitude as it is a skill level. Some people experts or businesses call professionalism as a way that we look or behave, yet it is far more than these components that make one a professional. Keep in mind that professionalism is most crucial and is an approach not just a job description. All qualities are formed in the way we think. Professionalism is very much in substantiation.

In order to cultivate the fruitages of self-improvement one must have willingness and put forth the effort to take his or her stand. It is the only way that you can develop professional qualities and skills. Effort, willingness, and motivation will drive you to the corners of professional growth.

You can use the Internet to find many ways to improve your image. An image you develop will reflect on others and yourself. You will feel more confident, esteemed, and prepared to take on the world. Professional growth is a demand, so it is always best to get started early. You have inner strengths, including self-insight to help you advance in professional growth. Your insight is the image you create of the self. Use these images to view yourself standing in an expert pair of shoes. Continue walking down the learning path into the world of professionalism and carry forward until you take your last breathe. This is a long-term process in which you do not want to let up applying effort.

You can also visit your local library and find information that directs you in the right path to expert growth. The library is full of books, magazines, and other reading materials. The

Leadership:
From Ability to Credibility

concept is to continue learning. Because technology is always advancing, one should never let up on learning. It is the primary key that will drive you down the road to professional growth. To learn more go Online today and find articles, books, and other information so that you can learn more about self-development. Find your answers.

Answers in Self-Insight and Professional Growth

When it comes to trying to find the answers inside yourself, you have to dig deep into your soul and your mind to find the right answers you are looking for. It is a long process and no one will tell you that it is easy, yet you can accomplish much by putting forth effort. So let me tell you how you might to learn how to get started. You have to be able to take a long look inside yourself sometimes, this is not easy for anyone but in order to be able to find answers it has to be done.

Searching your mind and insight will help you to find your hopes and dreams as well as to feel motivated enough to make your wishes come true. This is all about finding yourself and makes you have a better insight of yourself.

Sometimes it takes some time to become someone in a professional stance but as you grow, you will find that it will be easier for you to handle your responsibilities. This will help you to be able to define who you are and what you want in life as a person. This may help you to become a successful businessperson. In order to become a professional you have to work at it. This is not going to be something that does not take any time or effort; this is going to be an ongoing duty.

Sometimes people will experience some hard time but you will have to learn how to overcome this and walk through it. You will not only cross over discrepancy but you will come across many self-emotions and experience the power of self-growth. You may feel anxiety, fear, resentment, guilt and a lot of uneasiness. However, when you are feeling this way all you have to do is to learn to overcome it and move forward, you do not want to go backwards that would be defeating the whole purpose of what you are trying to do.

How does one get on the right path? Well it is totally up to you. It will all depend on you and your mind frame on how fast you will progress. It is going to take some time but as you learn to work on it, it will come to you faster than someone who only thinks they want it. This is going to take some time you will have to work at this every day until you get what you want or in until you are happy where you stand. However, you will find out you will also have to work at this all the time. In order to become that successful person that you want to be, there is work that you are going to have to do.

Some of the things that you may have to do to get where you want to be by sitting down and

Leadership:
From Ability to Credibility

making creating some goals. It does not matter how long they are or how short they maybe. Once they are down on paper, then you are going to have to learn to work at achieving your goals. You could even hang them in the kitchen since everyone goes to the icebox for something. This way you can see them and read them each day to keep your mind fresh. When you recently read something, it will soon sink in and this will make it so that you will always be working on your goals. Once you have your goals you will see that the rest will come, natural to you and it will help you to become a very successful person in life. Always keep it real!

Keep It Real with Self Insight and Professional Growth

Once you have decided what you want in life with your career that is you are going to want to make sure you keep everything fresh in your head. Therefore am going to tell you a few things that might help you to do that. Just think of how hard it was to get your professionalism status that you wanted so think how easy it will be to keep it.

There are many things that are available to you that you can do to help you to keep your professional status alive. What you have to do is research so it can help you to learn more as well as to keep up with all the new technology that is coming out every day. It don't matter if you're a mailman or a daycare provider there are always

Mark Zupo

news way that are there to try to make it bigger and better for you.

How do go about learning how to keep up with technology. There are always classes that you can take to keep your mind fresh of all new things that they are coming out with. You should always take some kind of refreshing class to help you so that you are not too burned out on your career. Sometimes you may have to take a major class to keep up with all the support that you need to be able to carry this out.

You have weakness where we do not want to do anything or to go on with life but we have to it is called life. Then again, we have strengths as well. These are what keep us going and going to where we are today with our learning and successes though out life in general. It is very important to figure out a way to keep your profession and to make sure that you say happy doing it.

Leadership:
From Ability to Credibility

CHAPTER 7

Strengths and Weaknesses

How do you keep your strengths and weakness?

It is hard to be able to keep your strengths if you do not do something about it. You have to be able to learn all you can even when you are feeling like there is no hope, there is always hope. Do not give up keep going until you are unable to go any more. We have all ran into major roadblocks but as you see if I let that stop me you would not be reading my article today. So keep your head up how and go as far as you can to make it happen for you in life. When it comes to your weakness you may have to pick, your head up high and do not look down it that is what is wrong with you. Then again, you may want to think about another profession if this one is getting you down and out. If there is just way around it and you have to do what you have to do. You do not want to get to the point that you have to go to the doctors to get help for this you need to try not to let this get you down and out to that point.

How would one go about find help to keep things fresh?

Well most of that have a profession know when we are getting down and out or that we need to take a refreshing class that will help you. You will have to do some researching and see what is out there for you. This may take some time doing. Some things that you may want to try would be talking to your follower employees to see how they manager there feeling or how they deal with the stress of the career.

Wonders in Self-Insight and Professional Growth

Have you often wonder what you were going to do when you were out on your own. It is very scarcely to be out on your own for the first time. this is why you have to decided what you want to do with your life do you want to make something of yourself or do you want to just be what you can well you can be what you want in life. Building professionalism is a great job, which you can pass onto your children. Now days there is so much going on with the world there isn't no jobs or no money to support yourself that is hard to go anywhere in the world this days so that is why there is schooling for the ones that what to do something with their life.

You have to be able to decide what you want to be and do it, in order to do it you are going to have to do some things to get started. Like being able to do some soul digging and looking into your life and as a child to see where you want to be in the next five to ten years. For some of this is going to be hard to do and for others it will not be a hard thing

Leadership:
From Ability to Credibility

to do at all. There is much to consider when you want to get out of the nest and make it on your own. So take some time and do that digging and find what you want in life and go for it, do not stop in until you reach your goal.

You will need to set goals. In order to set goals, you will need to have to search your mind. Dig deep in your mind to find out what you want to become. It is not easy to find good paying jobs these days unless you have education, experience, and professional qualities and skills.

If your wanting a good job you're going to have to learn a few things that might help you alone the way like how to self-examine, how to learn how to be able to concentrate on what is coming your way, as well as learning some new learning called subliminal learning. Self-esteem is essentially one of the qualities needed to improve professional growth. We all have to have good self-esteem in order to get anywhere in the world today. Self-esteem is the foundation of that builds sense of worth and self-respect.

So know that you have learned how to make you learn better as well as feel better lets go into the inner self and learn how to decided what we what to become in life. This should not be hard for some of you then again for some it going to be a challenge. We need to get started the first thing we have to figure out is what we want to be when the time comes do you want to be someone that is very professional like a doctor or a nurse or someone that might ran the world or do you just want to be a worker that gets by. We all have to make this decision in like and for some it is hard to do. With the right teaching and techniques, we all can make it happen. Do not rush take your time and it will come to you if you really want it to and you will get what you want out of life. You have the inner power; simply take it by the hand and move ahead to brighten your future. Conduct research today to find out what is available to you.

Research your Insight and Professional Self-Growth

Research will help you to improve your knowledge and skill when it comes to in-sight and professional growth. Finding the way!

When you want to improve your skills what do you have to do one of many things right. In order to get to the point that you want to be at you are going to have to dig for the information that you need but want as well. If you want something bad enough you will be able to get what you want it is going to take some time and work as well. Remember when it comes to improving your skill there is nothing easy about it. You are going to have to read, read, and work what you read. But reading is not the only way that you will be able to learn how to improve your skill there are a lot of ways that you will be able to too you will just have

Leadership:
From Ability to Credibility

to find the way that works best for you.

Some other ways that you can learn to improve your skill could be talking. Ok your thinking talking we talk all the time every day all day long will we are improving our skill we learn something new all the time and don't even realize it. Every time someone talks to us, we are learning something it may not be something good but we are learning. Just thing about it when someone tell us there name we have just learned there name what a fun way to learn about someone is though talking. Therefore, we have learned that we can learn from reading and talking to people. However, as we probably know that is many other ways that we learn. We can also learn from making mistakes, learning from our mistakes is a hard way to learn but we all do learn from them.

How would one go about learn how to learn new skills? If you would like you can also go and visit your local college they have people that are going though class that teach them how to open there possibility that will teach you how to do this. However going to college is very costly. However, there are grants that will help you with the financial part. There are classes that you can take to become very professional in whatever career that you would like to become. All you have to do is to dig inside yourself and decided what you want to become and go for it. It is going to be a hard for some but for the others it might be easy. Ok so what is the hold up? No one is ever too old to go back to school and continue learning. You will learn will learn something all though your life.

If you have a computer readily available, you can learn from that as well. You can enroll in online courses so that you can continue learning, build hope, and professional skills. This will help you a great deal the comforts of home while you learn that is so Kool. If you do not have a computer you can always go to your local library, they have a center of computer that they make available for your needs. There are ways to learn how to become all you can be all you have to do is apply yourself and start to become that professional that you want to become. It can be anywhere, any time; it is all up to you and your wants in life. Start examining the self.

Examining Self-Insight and Professional Growth

Have you ever taken a long look in the mirror to see what you see? Well we all have at one time or another, while looking at yourself your looking within yourself this could be you trying to find answer to a problem that you have been able to find the answers to or maybe you just want to be able to find who you want to be. There is no reason for you to feel sad or embarrassed by this we all have done it in our time it normal. We must all dig deep within our self in order to find answers that help us to improve our quality of life.

Leadership:
From Ability to Credibility

For some of us that want to make something with our life's there are some things that we have to do, in order to be able to find our self we have to be able to understand the ways that we are thinking as well as feeling. So am going to talk about three main ways that we find who and what we are.

The first thing is self-examine this is where you go and do some soul searching and be able to find yourself. Once you figured out how to self-examine, yourself then you can move to the other areas like meditation this is where you learn to empty your mind and learn to relax your body. This will make it easier to be able to think more clearly as well as be able to make up your mind up with a clear out look in things; you can learn this task from books in your local stores or your local library.

Mediation is a self-teaching course if you use it in the right way it will help you when it comes to problems that you used to have a hard time dealing with it will be easier. Now you have to remember that you cannot learn this over night so take your time and really learn this as well as understand it, things will come to you more natural than before when it comes to problem solving or just be able to work out the ends of what may be upsetting you.

Subliminal learning is also a good thing to know how to use it or to be able to use it. We can use techniques, such as probing into the mind to study past events, experiences, and knowledge to see if anything is available to expand our growth. Learning from your past is very important.

You will also have to have good self-esteem in order to learn. So try to have good self-esteem when learning new things. Having a positive outlook on things will help you as well. Having good self-esteem will make it easier for you to learn how to make the right discussions in life. Having good self-esteem will also make you feel better about yourself. When you feel good about yourself, life goes a lot easier for you.

Once you have learned all these little things then you will be able to think more clearly as well as to be able to make you your mind on what and how you want to learn and to become more professional with your learning tasks. Becoming a professional is one thing but to be able to use it wisely in the work field is another thing so all this goes together hand in hand, once you have learned this, your profession will come to you. Right alone with the other entire task you are going to learn. You will learn a lot though out your life so why not learn the right way and get all you can get out of. Find your way to self-growth.

Finding Self-Insight and Professional Growth

When it comes to trying to find yourself, you are going to have to take a trip. This trip can be anywhere you want it to be. For some of us we have to go to our local library or even go and play

Leadership:
From Ability to Credibility

on the computer. How is the computer going to help us we it will there are all kinds of information on the computer that will help you when it comes to trying to develop your professional skill to become someone successful. Your local library will help you as well they have material on all of the tips you may have to have to get started on your new life.

Your thinking I do not have a way to get around well there are dial rides that will help you get to where you need to go. If not then you might want to get a bike this will be great way for you to get your daily exercise. By the time you get to the library to get on the computer or to get that information that you want, you will have a clear mind making thinking easier for one to do. This is always good for one to do always enter the gates to success with a clear mind. So your thinking how do I get started doing this right well am going to take you on a trip to your local library so get your shoes and grab your coat and we will be on our way.

Study and read at the library so that you have a peaceful environment for learning. What a great feeling this is. No noise to get us sidetracked why we are working. We have to be able to get on the computer but just our luck they are taken. That is ok we will do some research on your own with the martial from the library that is offered to us. How do you do this there are computers that only work the library you will have to get on it and type in different keywords that will help you to find it in the library.

What are key words these are little words that will help you to find that special information on the subject that will help you. For example, you might want to punch in professional career; this will take you to all the information that will be able to help you with your professional career. This could be information on how to become a professional at a special career, or maybe give you information on how to become professional businesspersons will be all kinds of information on this in the area that the computer took you to.

Now let us go to the computer there is a spot open for you. You will have to sign it that is the first thing you will have to in order to be able to surf the internet. When you are surfing, the internet there is a lot of way to do your subject. There are a few different sites that you can also go to get information that will help you, the way that you surf the internet is by using different keywords. The way you do this would be to type in professional growth or maybe just professional this will get you started once you get started the information would take you all over the internet. You will find that searching for the information that you need, will be fun and easier than you ever thought. Find your way to professional growth with self-insight. Find your solutions.

Leadership:
From Ability to Credibility

Solutions

Self-insight is the process or technique we can use to look inward and analyze our feelings, thoughts, and behaviors. It enables us to move toward professional growth, which is the process that takes us to the development of skills to become sufficient in the workplace. Instead of lacking skills, we can look within the internal self and find answers that will help us to resolve the many problems one may face by finding answers. This builds the decision-making skills that we need to become effective pros in the work field.

Professionals are self-sufficient people that become certified specialist in a particular work environment. Their focus is often set on handling assigned tasks that they are qualified to manage. Instead of going through extensive training and education, some professionals take the hard course home to develop their skills by using self-insight. Although most professionals have to go thought some kind of training or schooling to be able to help the ones that are in need. Although there are some professionals that have learn just by looking though there insides and learning from that. Being able to look inside of yourself and teaching yourself how to become a professional without any, kind of course is very hard to do.

If you need to learn how to go about taking

some kind, of course, you will have to more than likely get in touch with your local college in your area they will be able to help you out. All kinds of programs out there will help you if you find that you need help paying for the training that you may have to have.

However, in order to do something like this you are going to find what you what to become. This is going to require you to do some soul searching as well as mental searching to make sure what you what to become is going to make you happy. This does not mean that you have to make up your mind today or in the next month; you can always change your career although some careers take longer than others as well as have different courses that you may have to take.

When you want to become a professional in a work field, you have to realize that is going to be hard as well as very stress full so you need to make sure you are up to this. Many jobs today require that you have a degree before they will hire you into the position. Some other jobs do not require a degree, yet the pay is minimal. Is ok if you find out later in time that it is not for you not is ok there are many professionals out there something will be there for you. just keep plugging and one will come to you if you really want this then if will easy for you to look inside yourself and find out want you really want to be and go for it.

Leadership:
From Ability to Credibility

If you find that, you will do better in your home there are colleges that will let you do your learning at home. This great way to get started you will be able to have some peace in your soul where you are in your own surroundings. There are some people that learn better in their own surroundings then in a big school, then again there are some that learn better in school this way there is help no matter where they may go someone is always around that can help. Therefore, this depends on you and your self-insight on how you want to learn to become a professional. What type of attitude do you have?

Mark Zupo

CHAPTER 8

Attitude and Insight

The Attitudes in Self-Insight and Professional Growth

Your attitude on life has a lot to do with the way things go for you. It hard to say that but it is so real. If your sad and feeling down it will make you not want to go anywhere in life like to be able to get a good career to even be able to stand on your own two feet. It seems like there are many people that have attitudes about something in life. This is particularly true when it comes to your career or job. You need to know that once you successes there will be the emotions, motives, and social psychologists attitudes that will come with this. You will have to decide which one is the attitude between your feelings and objects.

If you have a bad outlook on life you are not going to go anywhere in life. You have to have a positive attitude on life in order to do something with your life. For some of us the attitude that we carry is due to the way we have been treated though out our life's this will make a big difference in the way we perform on an everyday base. On the other hand, how we try to make our decision on a professional stand. We have to try to have a good outlook on life in order to be able to have a good

Leadership:
From Ability to Credibility

health life with our home and work area. Having a native attitude on life is going to make us have negative actions, which will cost us in the end with life as well as our career.

How does your attitude play a role in your life?

When you do not have a good attitude or viewpoint on life, things get rough often. Your attitude just does not affect you but everything around you. Your attitude and viewpoints reflect on others, and yourself. Changing your attitude is not an easy thing it something that is going to take some time with. You can change it with some will power a lot of will power you have to learn to reprogram you mind to work different this is going to take some time doing. It did not get that way over night so do not think it's going to just go away like a headache it don't work that way.

If you know anything that when you have a attitude at work it going to carry over to when you are at home as well as others are going to have one toward you. Therefore, if you are realizing this now then it is time to change your ways and do something about it.

Should you be afraid to change your ways.

No, you should never be afraid of change, since it is a growing tool. You want to change negative thinking and behaviors in order to create a professional attitude. That is many of the people problems today they are in fear of changing for the better. Then again, if they are not careful it can backfire on them as well. They can be giving as well as being mixed messages to themselves as well as to others. Fear of changing is sometimes a good thing and then again, it can be bad for us as well. Therefore, we have to learn how to use it. Rather than focusing your energy on the negative, center in on the positive.

When you make positive changes, it advances you, your skills, and qualities so that you can wear that professional attitude reflectively. Go online to learn some ways to make constructive changes today.

Viewpoints

We must consider the application of mental makeup and compare it to workplace behaviors, which comprise of human responses, discernment, divergence, partiality, and stereotype to understand the workplace behaviors and how they relate to professional growth.

Professional growth and issues in the job place link for the reason that each human's original thought play into the development of how one understands. Conceptions is a organization that materialize from an assortment of ideas, philosophy, viewpoints, thoughts, empirical

Leadership:
From Ability to Credibility

behaviors, impersonation from others, hypothesis, opinions, role models (influences), observation, beliefs, and take shape in a way in which a individual sees things as being veritable or what this entity may understand as being factual. This is the conceptual points to recall when you strive to use self-insight for professional growth.

Perceptions or assessment on the other hand comes from knowledge from observation and conscious discernments, or interpretations. It is the way one sees things, or hears words that establish that something is authentic or false. Because of observational interpretations that take shape from formed opinions, or someone reading too little or too much into something, often misconceptions develop. The interpretations, words, or reading messages in between the lines factor into how one perceives or thinks. Because we know that comprehension and perceptions factor into how one sees things to be absolute, we also know that to understand the sociological discerning is essential to give explanation to the social problems that take place in the workplace and how they relate to professional growth and self-insight.

Psychologists examine self-insight and professional growth in one way, while sociologist on average employs the hypothesis methods to associate the theories to sets of logical associations to testimonial, which may make an effort to illustrate, envisage, and/or give reasons for any social events that correlate to human behaviors. By understanding this formation and learning the characterization of human behaviors, perception, divergence, preconceived notion and stereotype, one can understand how issues in the workplace relate to the many problems we face today.

 Because of these issues, a high demand is in order to encourage all people to use self-insight in order to advance their professional growth. We all must work toward a new way of life by putting effort into reforming the way we think about the self and others. This is important when it comes to accomplishing professional growth. Because human behavior shows a discrepancy from entity to individual, divergence inside the workplace, continue living. The human behaviors are an outcome of both genetic, biological and situation – our biological want for survival and flourish can straightforwardly cause contention in the midst of co-workers."

 By reforming your viewpoints or self-insight, you can reshape the way you think, feel, or express yourself in a professional environment. It is the only way that you will make it through professional growth. Changing the way you see the world and others will help you develop social skills, which are so desperately needed in the business world. When you have good social skills, it makes it easier to interact with others without sweating the small

Leadership:
From Ability to Credibility

stuff, such as bias, or stereotyping. In fact building social skills alone will advance you to professionalism while reducing the stress. When you think positive, it reduces stress in many ways.

Thus, take professional growth by the horn today and move toward a better tomorrow. Professionalism in short term is success. If you want success, you have to work hard, think positive, and keep reaching, or climbing that ladder until you arrive at victory's door. Once you make it to this door, the key will be waiting for you to continue opening more doors.

Issues

We all face many challenges daily, which make it difficult for anyone to stay focused, positive, and to worry about develop professional growth. We all face the biological characteristic of life including war – all people are influenced by warfare and it shows in their behaviors. We also deal with various economical problems, such as unemployment and poverty. Despite that these issues exist, we still must stay focused however. Many people are discouraged from the leaders and government parties who are stealing their freedom each day.

Communism is other issues that affect our life, which includes racial strife, energy crisis, and so on. Budget deficits are declining. This is leading to the declining in morality and familial values. Many people fear the potential risks of warfare and terrorism attacks. Other issues include drug abuse, human and drug trafficking, in which all these issues affect our life.

Deficiency, and homelessness – corruption, aggression, declines in ethical and principles, as well as fairness is affecting our life and economy each day. Economy issues, such as gun and gun control, as well as energy crisis also affect our lives. Between 1965 and 1975 the tolls on cost-effective problems, such as privation and idleness was at 15% and 22 percent. The increasing figure goes, from bad to worse over the years, which the existing statistics reach well over 30%.

We see a need to make changes. We all must look in the mirror, looking deep within to see what changes we need to make. We can only change ourselves, so it is important to focus on you when you work toward professional growth. Socialism, such as cultural strife reached to 8% and 14% throughout the years, very little modification are made that give good reason for the inclining toll of problems we all face today. Racial discrimination is one of the foremost issues that we all must sort out and we are influenced by this hate in our workplace, schools, and other areas around the world.

Human behaviors are the way one behaves, which these responses reflect on our self-image and on others. Psychology spectators define behaviors as the way one behaves or responds to specific set

Leadership:
From Ability to Credibility

of conditions. Along these lines, we see that influences tap into how one reacts. For this reason, we must focus on the development of social skills while observing, and maintaining a healthy influential life while associating with other people. We need positive people in our life to make it to professional growth.

The psychodynamics interplay with our mental responses. It determines the way we think, feel, or wish for something. It connects us with the mind or way of thinking that we establish. It directs us to see that behaviors take place from mental proceedings. External regions of our consciousness also tap into this proceeding and our mental processes often will conflict with one another, especially if we do not take the time to reprogram the mind to abandon misconceptions. To become a professional thinker, one must leave behind childish thinking, or feelings, such as bias, stereotyped ways or thoughts, and so on.

Do not continue being part of life's problems; rather become parts of a solution that will make your life more fulfilling. Professionalism will drive you down the long-winding road to success. Yet, you must continue to put forth effort, applying yourself each day to reach and stay on this road.

Learning is a part of life. This part of life will

help you to abandon or leave behind any misconceptions that get in the way of your progress. Take some time to read articles and other information online to find ways to reach professionalism. How does behaviorism play into the workplace professional world?

Behaviorism

What is behaviorism and how does it affect one's ability to work toward professional growth?

Behaviorism is a study in non-analytic psychology in which approaches are used during study to concentrate on exclusive observation and to measure and modify behaviors. Materialist is the philosophical theories that make statements in relation to the mind and mental processes or states and what they are truly about or can become. Behaviorist typically view behaviorism in many ways and will consider the perceptions that form. The experts use various approaches and techniques to study human behaviors. In this instance, psychology concentrates on fashionable observations that facilitate them to appraise and transform behaviors. To the materialist – truth-seeking spectator, behaviors are declaration of the mind and mental states, which something is authentic or potentially being true.

Centrally, Freud made some of the best points when he give a rough idea of behaviorism, which was announced in the *psychodynamics and*

Leadership:
From Ability to Credibility

dynamics: Psychodynamics embroil the connections of emotional forces in which the emotions stimulate one to take action in a way that they may not usually conduct one self. This inner force derives from the subliminal system of the mind, which is generally referred as the subconscious mind. For a deeper understanding, one would have to probe into this mind to make new discoveries.

Rooted in the subconscious mind are divisions of our knowledge, recollections from precedent events, experiences, and so forth. Understandably, if you make a mental note of this district of the mind you will find that it has hidden messages that can impel you to discover ways to understand, acknowledge and find productive ways to reform or restructure your thinking and behavior, you would appreciate that this has all to do with the way one behaves. In spite of everything, it does not surge into the theoretical grounds, which are the original central theme of forming behaviors, thoughts, and so forth.

As said by (Nichols, 1972), the "silent, cataleptic dialogue" flood from our "higher-sense-perception" (HSP) and the experiences in which are "testimony, it becomes apparent that a soundless exchange of ideas (unconscious conversation) goes on biologically" in the midst of the "higher self," and with others. Nichols tells us "if this silent, communication come to pass at the height of conscious knowledge, it may come as an extrasensory perception, metavision, thought transference, metaudition, or presentiment. In spite of that what does this have to do with the problems in the administrative center?

Behaviorism affects our life, which if one has some faulty behaviors it could make it difficult to advance toward professional growth. Using your self-insight you can reflect on how you view yourself and work to make necessary changes to reform your behaviors and thinking. This will move you closer to professional growth.

When you take action, it helps you to make the adjustments you need to improve your skills. This is what professional growth is all about, self-improvement. If you want to get on the road to success, you must take action and work hard each day until you reach your goal. Keep in mind however, that professional growth is a lifelong adventure and you must stay on track.

Because behaviorists and materialist as well as many others are centering their attention on professional growth, this is becoming one of the most needed elements in our life. Due to technology advancements taking place each day, it is also required that we all advance toward professional growth. Use the Internet to learn more about behaviorism, professional growth; and how to use self-insight to make it happen. Get started today.

Leadership:
From Ability to Credibility

Understanding the function of distinctive branches of professional growth and self-insight

We can evaluate the natural environment viewpoint of behaviors, as well as the ways it affects our life every day. In keeping with the nature of sciences, this is one of *the largest part of dramatic* manipulate influences that have an effect on our mental process. For the reason, the point of view established by primitive philosophers lead behaviorists to analyze the issues further and then to was to reconcile the argument by questioning the area under discussion more systematically and methodically.

Delving into the sciences of behavior, behaviorists employed a collection of approaches, which commence with using appropriate course of action of "conducting psychological research" that cool, calm and collectedly went into a "meticulous concentration of the systematic" line of attack, which became the forerunner that guided them to look at carefully scientific structures and the experiments.

Scientists have used many techniques to analyze behaviorism. This is due to the many problems that people have with developing professionally through self-insight. One of the tests was the diametrically scientific observation of a rat.

This rat was encouraged to run through a mesh, or maze. During the test, the suckling was attached to a synthetic nipple. This was to help him make a "movable turn" during the test. The results showed that the heart rate inclined during the sound of a signal, or bell. It was noted however that before the test started that the suckling was given electric shocks.

Many experts thereafter claimed that none of us has the capability to observe direct cataleptic purpose or motive. Because of the results many scientists and behaviorists paved the way to developing other scientific applications. The standardized applications are regulated and enables scientist to compare similar behaviors through observational learning.

Some believe that these predictable test results can be used as an example to help people work toward professional growth by using self-insight. Evolutionist use some of the same applications, which has became one of the most essential solutions that has helped scientists find reason to justify the facts revealed. The applications used over the years to explore human behaviors have directed many others to study the chief sub-disciplinary structures in the psychology, as well as in the workplace. These biopsychology studies reach into human behaviors and mental processes in order to help experts and others to examine the physical foundations, which cause stress that

Leadership:
From Ability to Credibility

develops from thoughts and targets the emotions.

In the social channels of psychology, as well as in the clinical and cognitive, the focus here channels into professional growth and into the work fields. This is the I/O or the industrial and organizational sectors, as well as the health, educational, and other applications that are applied in the studies to help scientists and others to understand human behaviors. In today's business world requirements are setup in various companies putting more emphasis on the need to develop professional skills and qualities. Essentially, more and more companies are putting up higher demands in order to create a harmonized and structured environment. For this reason, many people are considering continuous education in order to continue learning and meet the requirements imparted to them by various organizations around the globe.

Japan is one of the major areas in the world that expects professional attitudes in the work field. China and Tokyo is another area that has a high demand placed on professional growth. This pattern is spreading, which in time, every corner of the world will require that people focus on using self-insight for professional growth. What are the ratifications?

Ratifications

Mark Zupo

When you want to be able to make changes, you have to be able to a have a positive attitude. A positive attitude will help you when you feel worn out from making all the necessary changes to improve your professional growth. When one has a negative attitude then they will have a bad attitude toward life and everything around them. Therefore, we have to learn to get rid of the negative thinking so that we can have a positive attitude toward life as well as be able to make our self-feel better so that we can make a better life for us and the people that we love.

Do you realize that your physiological performance has a reflection on the mental and emotional attitude? With this attitude, it will help to develop how well you see things that reflect on the way you feel about things in your life. We deliberately use our critical and the thinking abilities that can and will reflect our ways of actions as well as the accomplishment and the way that we succeed in life.

We have to learn to get off the couch stop being those nice little couch potatoes, when someone is lazy it will or could affect the way they think as well as have a reflection on our actions and make it hard to be able to be successful in the world today. Our attitude is mostly developed by how you see things. If we learn how to take actions on how to have a positive attitude, it might lead us to become successful in one's life. For this reason, we need to cultivate a positive attitude and

Leadership:
From Ability to Credibility

maintain our position.

Here are some negative reflections that we may want to look at. These will help us to figure out what we have to do for our self in order to get successful. Some of the things that we need to look for would be confusion, agitation, feebleness, senile, overwhelming stress, victim of the bad and easy prey. Here are some of the positive reflections would be accomplishment, active, regal, accepted, leadership, motivated as well as energized and being in control. This will help you to become successful in your life as well as to learn how to get in control of your actions. Your attitude depends on you, as a person you can have a good outlook on life or again you can have a poor outlook the way that you see things is the way that you feel. So if you have a good outlook on things you will feel a lot better. The way you feel and your look play a big part on your success in life and in your profession growth.

How are we going to learn how to deal with this what can I do to make it happen?

The first thing you have to do is to go deep inside yourself and decided why and how to change. In order to do this you are going to have to sit down and really think about if you want to change there are many ways to change your ways. It is up to you to decide how to do it. In addition, you need to remember that it is not going to be instant; it is going to be something that is going to take some time and effort in doing. Therefore, this is going to all depends on you and your well power on how fast you make it to where you want to go in life.

Problems

We often think that we are something, with our little attitudes that is many of the problems today is people that have attitudes that make life harder than they should be. It is hard to say for sure, since everyone is different. Now days people think that they do not have to do anything about anything it comes natural. Well the ones that think this is so wrong this is not something that comes to us we have to work at it. Therefore, we all have to be able to learn how to work at this and in this passage, we are going to talk to you about learning how to have a positive attitude to help us to be able to get what we want in life. When we are able to get what we want in life, it will help us to become that professional that we want to become. This will also help you to have a better self-insight on yourself and others around you. Many people struggle with finding the right pathway to reach their destination. Well let me tell you something is that might be of some help to you.

Here is something that might be off some help to you. You could try some mediation this is a self-teaching course that will help you to learn how to be able to clear your mind of all things. Mediation is been around for years so it must work

Leadership:
From Ability to Credibility

they are using it all around the world to help them to get though some of the hardest times in life. Using this technique will build your confidence and self-respect. We all need to learn how to respect our body we need to know how to do the same to our minds and souls as well. When we are learning to mediated, we will learn all of these things to help us.

If you find that meditation is difficult for you, perhaps you can try yoga. Yoga is a guide that takes you to develop professional skills and qualities. It is a self-disciplinary action. Yoga is an excise that teaches you to learn to breathe as well as relax your mind and your body. Yoga has been a practice that many people all over the world has used over the centuries to develop professional skills. There is information all over the internet. Just get on the computer and go surfing to see what you can find. If you are not able to find anything on the internet then you might want to try to go to your local library they have martial on the subject there alone with the history of it.

We all need to learn ways to develop a positive attitude when it comes to professional growth. With all the studies that are out today, we can learn how the body work and what we can do to help us to reduce the rise of a short life. They have found out that when a person thinks with a positive attitude that they will live a healthier and happier life. Did you know that staying in a positive stage this would prolong the aging processes? This will also enable us to be able to focus what make us strong or be in a negative stage of thinking that will cause us to have weakens in our life's. Once you decide to make constructive changes, it will change your overall quality of life. You have to be able to imagine yourself in the moment so that you can focus on what you need to do to accomplish your goals. Except change:

Change

You have to be able to examine them on a daily base. We all have natural ways to improve our life. Some of these techniques include self-talk or self-analyze. Listening to the inner voice will help you to develop a positive attitude. It will guide you down the road to success. When you have developed you new attitude on life you will feel better, look better and be able to perform better making you function better make it easier for you to be able to success in your life.

When we experience our emotions and attitude, one can only reflect with a positive way of thinking making them stay stronger and healthy. When aging starts, the body goes through many changes. The changes often reflect on your responses, attitude, and will increase your stress level. You may start to feel down. Some things that you have to do is be able to fight off this feeling like being able to exercise, eat healthy and be able to have a clear mind to be able to focus on the

Leadership:
From Ability to Credibility

positive future that is coming your way. This is a hard thing to do at times but it can be done if you work at it all of this will help you to have a better in-sight on yourself and have a better outlook on life in general.

We have to remember that our success comes from positive thinking and positive actions that we are always working on. We are in great hopes that we will be able to learn though the patterns and actions that our lifestyle brings us. I hope that these things will help us to be able to be encouraging us enough to be able to reprogram the way we think and feel. All of this will help us to be able to keep in touch with all of our reality making this a fun learning advancer.

We have to be able to work at this everyday all day long even the people that do not have a problem they have to work at this as well. This is something that has to be done every day of our life in order to become something that we are all capable of doing. With a little work, this can all be taken care of its nothing that we cannot do if we put our minds together we can do anything. This is something that we are all capable of doing. Again, you have to be willing to work at it. Its wont just comes to you it is going to take some work and affect.

Attitudes play a great deal with your everyday living you may not think it does but it does. If you wake up mad or just in a bad mood you're going to have a bad day all day most of the time this is how it works there might be some times when it don't and that is a good thing. Your attitude plays a big deal on the development of your conception, perceptions, as well as your influences that display from our feeling and emotions. This is the way that one feels when something or someone has hurt them or causes any reflection on their life and on others. There are three areas of the brain that function as a part of this they are the conscious, unconscious, and the subconscious mind. These will help to teach and help to display our feeling and emotions.

The conscious, unconscious as well as the subconscious mind is common used to explain the attitudes that we have. These all play on whether you have a positive or a negative outlook on life and determine the attitude that you have. It guides you to develop a positive attitude or negative attitude, which you must take control in order to redirect your mind when it switches to negative. Do not let the shadows follow you into self-defeat.

Shadowing

Your attitude is something is carried with you throughout your life and is reflected on you and everyone around you so you should think about this if this is a problem for you. Your attitude will go everywhere that you go; it is like your shadow so if you think you may have a problem with this then

Leadership:
From Ability to Credibility

you may want to try to do something about it as soon as you are able to do it. Your attitude will go with you with your work as well as your life style. The way your thinking reflects on others could put a dent in your professional life.

When trying to change your attitude you have to work at it. It will take some time, but can be done. With some time and a little studying, you will soon see a change your behavior. Times are hard as you already know this and with you having an attitude, it is just going to be that much harder on you. Therefore, if you are able to do something about it you should. Having a good attitude will help you to have a better outlook on life in general.

When wanting to know if you have a positive outlook on things you need to be able to scale your feelings as well as your emotions, right along with your thoughts. This will make you be able to see things with a different eye. When having a positive attitude it is related to your mental states of mind. This will help you to get all your feeling, morals, and disposition in the right way when it comes to your thinking and speaking and help with your behavior that you have.

There is evidence out there that will help you to see that when one improves there psychological and physiological states that they will feel a lot better. The higher state of mind that you may have will help you to improve your health as well. When you are feeling better about you it will lower your risks of heart disease, the stress levels in your mind and body, as well help you with your immune system this will help to decrease the risk of death.

There is a lot of reason to try to change your attitude on life for it will be easier for you to success in life with what you want as well be healthy for you when it comes to your health. Finding the way to living healthier is a type of insurance that you will make it through professional growth.

Take some time to search the Internet to find ways to use insight to manipulate through the growth phase to arrive at the door of professionalism. This is a requirement these days, so be sure to get on the road as soon as possible. You will improve your life, make more money and welcome positive friends into your life. Filling your world with positive influences makes it easier to carry the load or weight that life puts on your shoulders. Online you will find a wealth of the latest information that guides you in the right path to professional growth.

Look for the updated articles and read some of the older news to find techniques that help you make the most of professional growth. The information flowing online includes self-development, which are the steps toward professionalism. Be sure to read how others have worked through self-development to build their

Leadership:
From Ability to Credibility

skills and qualities. Build your willpower as well, so that you can flow inside self-insight to professional growth.

Flowing

We spend a lifetime trying to solve problems, and then another good part of our life trying to minimize the level of problems we are challenged with each day. It just goes to show that we must thrive each day to move through professional growth. Life never seems to give us a break at times. When we do get a break, we spend the time, trying to figure out how to use self-insight to work toward professional growth. Can anyone say, "Rollercoaster," ride! That is what life is all about.

Still, we must get on the rollercoaster and head toward the road that leads us to success. With the new changes in our workplace and environment, we must work diligently today to achieve our goals. We need to constantly learn, and strive to make it to the finish line. Finding links and information can help you make the goal line.

All through our lifetime, we often fall into the flight-by-fright stages, which take us from beginning to end to a high pollutant negative drive. This often tears down the positive thinking habits we had worked so hard to build up. We lose sight and focus, which makes it difficult to manage life, let alone our duties at our workplace.

Mark Zupo

Focusing on what you must do is a major part of advancing into the professional growth arena. When you are psychologically aware and can dissect the ways you manage life to reform your behaviors, you are heading down the right boulevard. Our line of attack or way of thinking factors into our conclusion; deplorably, most humans do not spend a good amount of time focusing on the bad things they do, or even the good things, rather they wait until the extreme is noted in their lives and associations, personal and professional, either constructive or negative."

Contented souls often set out to create a set of attitudes, which their actions, beliefs, thoughts, and learned behaviors start to structure. This all keys into the predilection and heredity and is a state of mind. One can stay focused on developing mind over matter. Before you take upon yourself to stumble into this neighborhood, however you need to understand what mind over matter means. This is the seat of our thoughts and memory that encircles the consciousness realization and produce our feelings, thinking, perceptions, ideas, etc, and then stores this information in a safe district to form as knowledge and memories. The level of thinking capacity is what determines what mind over matter produces.

Our constructive mind, make a replica of our memories and thoughts and is often formed from the laws of attractions. It is also fashioned from the power of thinking positive. What is more,

Leadership:
From Ability to Credibility

it forms in the way that one acts in agreement.

Hypothesizing this notion can smooth the progress of you seeing how you would act in response to words, actions, or things. You can question yourself to figure out what you learned, felt, thought, and so forth. Use your self-talk skills to question the self. Find out what you learn. These are only some of the ways to get on the road to professional growth. Learning what professional people develop can help you make improvements and move in the right direction. View some of the outlines below and analyze the traits in order to see how it can benefit them. Professionals develop positive-thinking habits, a higher plane of consciousness, self-resilience and will take control of their thinking, behaviors, and viewpoint on life. Professionals build self- confidence through self-talk Meditation and other techniques help them to cultivate skills, such as self-control. Find some links online.

Mark Zupo

CHAPTER 9

Links to Self Insight

Links in Self-Insight and Professional Growth

How to find the right links and information to perform with a positive attitude to help with professional growth as well as in-sight ---

As you already know that having, a positive attitude is not going to solve all of your everyday problems but it will help you to be able to solve them. When one has a good attitude it helps a lot when a problem comes about. Just think about it if you are not having a good day your attitude changes real bad right. When this happens your feeling all blue and down, but when you're having a good day your all happy and cheerful. this is not uncommon this is the way you are suppose to feel but you feel so much better on a good day then a bad day. Not one of us can say that we had not endured a bad day. Everyone has them and it entitled to them that is a given in life.

With this in mind, you are going to have to consider some flight-fright. This is the stage that where the negative and positive breaks. We have found out that if you stay focused on what is coming you will be more mentally aware this will make you more scrutinize with the positive ways of doing things. We all have to remember that our

Leadership:
From Ability to Credibility

attitude has a great deal of factors in our outcomes. Therefore, we should always start thinking of the good and good things will come to you.

This is really a good way to think when it comes to trying to find a job or to learn good things. Good positive attitude will help to be able to learn how to clear one's mind. When you want to be able to clear your mind of all things, you may want to try some mediation this work dearly.

You have to remember that you are not the only person out there that is feeling the way that you are feeling right now. Nevertheless, get up, brush yourself off, and get it together so that you are able to become that professional person you want to be or to get all that you can get from your self-insight. However you have to remember that its really going to take some time and affect this isn't nothing that you're going to see a big change overnight you will be able to see something soon but it all takes time when it come to this matter. So take your time and do the best you can learn all that you can there is plenty of information out there that will help you to learn this. The biggest thing is that you are going to have to take your time, put your mind to the change, and go for it.

Aspects

What we see as the perceived personality factors into the aspects of the ways that others perceive us as well. For instance, if you perceive yourself as a

King on a Throne," likely someone else may view you as a domineering person, except if you were enlisted as a King in a distance country where Kings and Queens exists.

If you perceive yourself as a computer whiz, yet do not have the skills people in time will start to see you as a liar. Of course, we can bring into play self-insights to generate a professional representation of the self, but one had better damn well have actions to back his or her claims. Or else, this one will become a fake, (Labeled by others) which very few people will like.

How creations from behaviorist approaches fits into insight and professional growth and the way we understand it today: We can take a behaviorist line of attack into the 20-centry to understand self-insight and how it can help one to build up professional skills through individual development. Pavlov (1849-1936) set the familiar sight when he conducted an experimentation involving a dog. At some stage in this experiment, Pavlov discovered that at what time one becomes accustom "to hearing an" explicit "sound" during dinnertime, or other mealtimes that this one will salivate naturally or biologically. Each time they hear the sound at mealtime, consequently the entity will salivate. Learning then supposedly formed the path for Pavlov, which he debated many points with other behaviorists? One of the debates was that animals, as well as humans behavior associates with "rejection." The behavioral pattern

Leadership:
From Ability to Credibility

according to some spectators is urbanized through learning.

The study took psychologists to examine and identify the biochemical alterations taking place within the brain cells, as well as the neural circuits that involve learning. These ideas were at risk however, simply because some behaviorists formed perspectives to eliminate the theory. Descartes one more of the behaviorists put much weight on the theory that knowledge stem "from experience," and is generated through our thinking processes. According to the philosophy of

Descartes, we all reproduce theories based on our experiences, and these reflections are used to develop "new insights about oneself," and the way one sees the "world." (Westen, 2005)

We have the states of two parts, which make up the body and mind. According to the theories of these two opposing conceptions, people make up two separating constituents, which include the body and the mind. These two constituents set the landmark for mental and physical events that have dividing cause.

The mind has the liberty to think as well as choose its path, while the body has limits, which conform to the basic "law of nature." According to these understanding, in order for one to employ his or her self-insight to cultivate the fruits of professional growth, thus one must rely heavily on the mind, since it empowers one to make choices and think.

Despite that these theories made some headway however and drifted into our future, the fact is other theories are explored, which after giving much consideration, one can then see how self-insight is our ticket to developing professional growth. Using our own insight from learning that drifted in from our experiences, one can focus on cultivating his or her professional growth. Yet, first, one must understand what it means to be professional. Thus one must focus on thoughts, feelings, actions, words, behaviors, and other specifics in order to pass the pro – scale that despite what others thinks, make you who you are. Go online to learn more. Learn how the cognitive mind works.

Cognitive Self-Insight and Professional Growth

Paving the way to better tomorrows, many spectators, dictators, opinionates, philosophers, writers, Talk Show experts, psychologists, and many others are calculating the ways one can use self-insight to move toward professional growth. Many of the ideas are streaming down the long-winding river of psychology whereas many environmentalist, behaviorists, scientists, cognitive processing, and other related persons with genius minds come up with various ideas that lead to the notions we see today. For example, under the study

Leadership:
From Ability to Credibility

of child development many scientific minds discovered that relevant influences fact in to how a child grows.

The cognitive perspective put much emphasis on the way that people perceived things; and processed the information; and where the information comes from. The roots of cognitive psychology has sent many experimental results upstream in order to make some valid points, which drifted us to self-insight and professional growth. Wundt is one of the entities of interest, which during the 19th century the examined the concepts of mystery or phenomena. These phenomena included influences, perceptions, and one's ability to "remember lists of words." (Westen, 2005)

During the experiments measurements were taking, which lead to the theory that perspectives take us through the process of thinking, retaining, and gaining information. Environmentalists put some words in on these theories, which lead us to believe that transformations stored information, and data retrieved uses a number of "mental programs," to process and interpret meaning. This ultimately leads to the basic responses that form through behaviors, known as output. Because of this basic knowledge, we see that how we perceive plays into how we react. Thus, we must use insight from within to find the way to developing the professional self. The mind is similar to a computer. That is the actions work in similar way.

Computer layout:

Housing or casing – keyboard (Input device) mouse (input device), monitor (Output/input device), Internal parts – mother board – the component that controls all units – modem (The device that controls and causes input/output from the Internet), video chip or card (The device that controls images), RAM (Random Access Memory) Hard Drive (Storage), Processor --- Hard Disks

---Hard disks are responsible for holding the primary memory. This memory is stored within a computer chip that sits on the computer's motherboard. The secondary storage unit is on the computer's hard drive. This drive holds important memory, which instructs the computer to take action.

How does this relate to insight and professional growth? The mind is similar to a computer processor and storage compartment. We have three areas of the brain, which include the conscious, unconscious, and subconscious mind. The conscious mind holds information that we learn through experiences, events, and knowledge gained. How much one retains information is based on; his or her level of reaching an understanding: how he sees things: how much his mind retains; and how attentive he was during the time of learning. We have the short and long-term memory that branches out from these areas, which the long-term memory is part of the memory that retains

Leadership:
From Ability to Credibility

one's experiences permanently; thus, this is your primary storage partition.

The short-term memory is your temporary storage screened-off area where information is stored for a short while. Like a computer, the primary storage partition branches off and functions alongside the (cylinders) cells, (Tracks), fibers, and so on. The hard drive is the electronic device, which reads/write whereas the heads pass back/forth over the cells, reads the information from the primary storage area, and then writes the information to this area of the brain. Now, if you want to use your self-insight to develop professional growth, thus, read and write from the primary storage while probing into the secondary storage partition to hunt for hidden messages that direct your path. Take the dip.

Dip into Self Insight and Professional Growth

How to relate to self-insight by examining the cognitive approach Revolutionary changes unfolded in the past three decades whereas new points were brought into focus by psychology studiers, experts, and scientists. For this reason, we often see cognition (the ability to acquire knowledge) which is the mental faculties or processes that acquire knowledge by using perceptions, intuitions, and reasoning. This process has taking the lead over the 20th century disputes and theories that lead to behaviorist approaches.

Mark Zupo

At one point, the C.E.O. workers aboard the psychology department were asked a question. The question revolved around cognitive approaches, which eight of the ten professionals agreed that cognition took the front. Many points has been issued that presented many views and questions.

Many of these questionable views stream from the Western Philosophers, (Philosophy of the mind) and (Sciences of the mind) and behaviorists (sciences of behaviors) --- (Westen, 2005)

Jean Piaget became a worth mentioning philosopher when she came up with the idea that cognitive perspective is the focus "on the way people perceive, process, and retrieve information." (pg. 15; Psychology) Jean's new finding led other psychologists and scientists to believe that memory structures encode the information we learn from experiences so that we can store it for later use and retrieve it when needed. According to Jean's discovery, our coding structure affects "how" easy "we can later access" the info that we retain.

Taking the dip into the mind, one may consider other aspects and theories, yet this idea led most people to believe that the human mind only functions on 10 percent of the 100% storage capacity. As humans, we typically retain numerical more so than we do names.

Taking the test:

555-8787

Leadership:
From Ability to Credibility

Green, Yellow, Orange, Purple, Black, Red,

Review, and try to remember these lists. Once you are finished, stop and close your eyes. Do not look at the lists again. Try to recall what you remember. Likely, you will remember the numbers, but will forget the list of colors. This is not a problem; it is just a point to be made. We have two sections of the mind, which is our long-term and short-term memory. The long-term stores permanent information, while the short-term mind stores temporary files. The mind stores information and enables us to use it when relevant questions are presented. The short-term mind cannot act as quickly to give us information because it does not connect us to direct environment; rather it links us to the past memories.

What is the purpose?

The purpose is if you intend to use self-insight to develop professional growth, thus cognitive thinking must be understood, since it gives way to the decision-making processes. For example, per se you stroll into a department store with the intent of buying a new Dovetail Fixture. The first thing you think of before you walk in the store is the fundamental characteristics that you want to find, such as price, style, features, quality, and so on. While you are working out the details in your mind, the salesmen is at the other end of the food chain calculating how he will describe the tool, how much the quality outweighs the cost, and so on. Both of you are dipping into the languages of knowledge. Each party is deliberating and wondering what the other one is saying, or meaning as both of you speak. The sales clerks for example, may say, "This is the bargain of a lifetime." You might interpret this as, "there is better deals elsewhere."

Now if you dip into your insight, you could compare and contrast the price, quality, style, and other characteristics, especially if you would have researched prior to stepping into this store. Now you must assimilate all aspects of the product, and then decide on its importance and partner that is buried deep in your mind, thus silently channeling information to help you make a decision, and is transmitted through the neural driving forces, i.e. your subconscious mind. Become the next leader.

Leaders in Self-Insight and Professional Growth

Taking the role of the leader is never easy. Leaders tend to bear more influence than a follower does. While leaders are great influences than common followers, leaders also have balance. We can review a few leaders that had balance and compare them to unbalanced leaders. One of the prime leaders of our time was Adolf Hitler. Adolf Hitler had great leadership skills, yet he took his beneficial skills beyond the limits and boundaries of humanity and straight into a holocaust of horrific

Leadership:
From Ability to Credibility

crusades of competition that lead to the death of millions. Adolf Hitler became infamous by arousing the attention of others and guiding them to following him to these rivalries. This is definitely a poor leader; despite of the attention he drew from others.

Factually, Adolf Hitler was one of the most prominent and intelligent human species that walked the face of the earth. Unquestionably, this man left bad imprints on the clean, ethical souls that understand that his intelligence was based on greed thus signifies him as one of the most stupid individuals that ever walked the planet.

One of our best examples of a leader is Martin Luther King, Jr. This fine man set out to reach his aspiration despite of the many obstacles that got in his way of achieving his goal. Mr. King obviously had a fine role model, his father, yet he also had refreshing morals, values, ethnics, ethic, and other clean standards that made him who he became. For this reason, we can use Mr. King as a fine role model to follow when we are striving to use self-insights to cultivate professional growth. Bill Clinton is another fine role model. Even though he endured trial and error before the public, Clinton continued to withstand his ground and show true leadership. Rather than conform to "norms," he ventured to show that all humankind despite of their color, culture, background, etc, could take the role as a leader.

Mark Zupo

Over the centuries, women had to struggle harder than everyone else to make their way into the human category. Sadly, women are still fighting today. Fortunately, however one of the best role models of our time Emily Murphy took the lead and became one of the primary female judges that fought to establish that Canadian Women were human beings "under the law." Some of the worst leaders then are seen in the district of the law, and in criminal justice. They took the lead and led many people into practicing bias, stereotype, hate, and finally into murder and crime. Check the history of the bible to clarify.

By scrutinizing these role models, one can weigh against and contrast the differences and see that a true leader is not biased, stereotypes, haters, players, unreasonable, doubters, ploys for argument, and so on. Rather a true leader is a pure, original person with high standards, values, and morale. A leader then has confidence, self-esteem, high spirits, drive, and aimlessly seeks to achieve his or her goals. If you use your insight, you will find that professional growth is just around the corners and success is about to happen. Everything is within reach; all it takes is you to get on the way to making it happen. Leaders are humble. Instead of assuming things will happen a true leader will make things happen. A person in charge is unassuming, self-effacing and someone that is subservient. A submissive soul many misconceive, as someone is self-sacrificing or a

Leadership:
From Ability to Credibility

victim. Contrary to these notions, a leader is submissive. A leader does not have a problem with letting others take the need, when the need is of great relevance and can benefit all.

Leaders create goals, plans, backup plans, and put forth the effort to make it happen. Instead of using insight that others help to develop, use your own insight to find your way through the professional growth world. You will see amazing differences in you. To learn more about professional growth and self-insight, visit the World Wide Web of Cyber confusion to find more answers. Do not forget to review the styles of a leader.

Styles in Self-Insight and Professional Growth

What are the styles of a leader?

Leaders are autocratic, laissez-faire, and democratic. (Self-governing, independent) The first style is someone that must make all decisions; the second is someone that involves self in-group activities while encouraging others to take the lead. This person will give other people right away to make his or her own choices. The democratic is someone that allows things to take place and will only intervene when he or she does not have other options.

The first leader type often products crafts. This leader often drifts off when superior leaders are not present. The products that he or she designs are often substandard compared to the democratic leader's designs. The democratic leader often finds a way to solve problems without using aggression or violence. In addition, this type will feel a greater sense of contentment. The Laissez-faire type rarely feels efficient or content. During studies, it showed that democratic leaders are both inspiring and competent. The Laissez-faire type has the capacity to be ecologically aware but not contented at the same time. The Laissez-Faire type is someone that is not the hands-on type, and someone that is unautocratic. They often are accommodating, lenient, nonjudgmental, and someone that is liberal.

Autocratic are often tyrannical. They repress and oppress others from taking the lead. These people can become overbearing, domineering, and unreasonable. This is the traits of a poor leader. Their dictatorial status makes them the high-hands in society that no one wants to meet or deal with, yet they are everywhere.

Democratic leaders are equal people that live under the self-rules of their own establishment. This type is likely to pursue professional growth by using his or her, own self-insight. Likely, this one will succeed. The autocratic on the other hand, despite of the many successes he may claim, in due time, this leader will fall flat on his or her face.

By considering the types of leaders, one can decide what type of leader he or she already is; and

Leadership:
From Ability to Credibility

then move to expand on his or her qualities and skills. During I/O studies, i.e. Industrial/organizational, scientists of psychology ventured to explore the types of leaders. Upon completing several experiments that soon learned that 2-D, i.e. dimensions played into guidelines of defining a leader's type. That is they considered the task and relationship point of reference.

Psychology basis its discoveries on measurement, divisions, contrast, logic, commonsense, and so on. These disjunctive divisions form as numbers, which the problems are then presented to attempt solving the most complex problems by considering the tasks. Along the lines of these tasks, each variant of the tasks are considered, which include: "Non-Eureka and Eureka." What this means is that we respond to something positive by expressing triumph. We express joy when we discover something new, find answers to problems, or succeed at completing a task.

    On the other hand, we roll back the rug and claim, here it is when we feel the Eureka spirit, yet when we feel the non-Eureka feeling, and often we feel little if any satisfaction. Usually, when we discover something, we often deliberate to see if it is true. The relationship and point of reference perceptions is based on the way we understand words, and how one leader differentiates. It is the focus of competence based on how the leader views the feelings of his or her workers.

This takes us above the limits of leaderships types, taking us into the cross fires of cultural, bureau agencies, and unity. Trust me; you do not want to be caught up in this cross fire until you start to see how styles of leaderships factor into using self-insight for professional growth.

Self-Insight and Professional Conceptual Growth

Do you sell yourself short? Do you often underestimate your abilities? If you do then perhaps you could use a lesson in developing societal cognition to exert the self through professional growth. Motivational and emotional development keys into develop social skills.

Many people struggle with interpersonal relationships because of the difficulties that occur, and often the causes are due to lack of communication. This is a professional skill one must develop in order to function on a multi-scale.

When one develops an understanding of self, as well as for others and works toward social development, often their feelings will change. This is all part of social cognition improvement. We can center on self-concept to decide what skills you need to build.

Self-concept is the way one perceives his or

Leadership:
From Ability to Credibility

her personality. It is also how someone else sees your personality. This step is the first task that you must use to work toward developing social cognitive skills. When you acquire a good sense of the self, and become aware of your distinctive traits and physiological qualities, as well as your mental processes, you are at a great stand in social development.

Innately, many people believe that have already established the way that they see themselves. This is not true. This is part of a development process that requires, practice, skills, and plenty of training. We must recognize that our feelings and thoughts belong to the self. From the onset of our birth, we start to formulate roundabout methods so that we can learn the steps through self-concept. After the first few years, we develop dependable processes in order to measure out level of development. Each one of us sees ourselves differently than others see us. By the time, we reach two-years of age we often compare the self to the way we become visible to the way; one should appear. This is the start of visual conceptions. After this, stage one move to examine the inner self.

The visual steps of building concepts take one though a categorization phase. At this time, the person starts to see the self on multifaceted dimensions. Children are highly keen during this phase. At all age groups past 2-years we have the ability to note discrepancy and consistencies in our behavior or attitude. By noting these changes, we often determine if we are extroverted or introverted. The underdeveloped souls in the world often find it difficult to use other than generalization in regards to their thoughts or feelings.

The immature might say,

"I hate this quality about me." The quality may be having the ability, such as multi-skill. This is a weakness and strength because this quality enables one to handle a wider range of tasks while using the left and right side of the brain. If this person was skilled at seeing the bigger picture, he might say, "I have a weakness and strength in my multi-tasking abilities, yet I can integrate these traits to create a unique way of managing tasks." This is a new version that does not oversimplify the individual.

The main thing here is to build professional qualities that enable you to look at the entire picture, rather than parts. At the age of eight, a youngling' often sees the self by tapping into the self-insight or internal being. Characteristics of our psychological makeup one is audible, which controls all aspects of one's cognition. In short, the person becomes aware of his or her dislikes and likes. Throughout the phase of growth, the person begins to think for his self and feel. We now can consider the way we view others.

Leadership:
From Ability to Credibility

Views in Self-Insight and Professional Growth

When it comes to self-development and understanding others, it is almost like a seemingly endless rollercoaster ride that never seems to stop. Just when you think you have figured out someone, new development stages unfold and you are back to learning again. When you work through professional growth by using self-insight, it pays to keep the golden rule in sight. "Just when you think you know it all, you soon find out that you know nothing at all." This is a never-ending cycle for all of us.

To understand others as well as the self, you must go through this permanent episode of changes and development. By the time you become a young one in the infancy phase, you already have a measure of achievements. This is part of the recognition of interacting sociably, which takes you to a mutual stand in growth. During this stage, infants tend to develop this view that their other individual dealings are based on the self.

We analyze perceptions. We carry on finding out how they play into using self-insight for professional growth, which also takes us around the circles of theorization that develops in the mind. Throughout adolescent and beyond we move into the "perspective-taking" phases, which drives us straight into the gutters of understanding one's ability to view others and the way they may see things.

Mark Zupo

We use visualization tactics to examine others and the self. Using these same tactics one can expand his or her professional growth through inner insight. Using visualization combined with affirmations we can clear any doubts from our minds. This includes self-defeating doubt, such as doubting one's ability to reach goals. We all have this ability. Some are sluggish, some of us miss the points, and some other of us makes it to the finish line. You want to be one of those on that finish line by develop professional skills.

We make to this line through training, practice, exertion, and using techniques that work for us. One of the best ways to get started is by assessing and measuring your weaknesses and strengths. You will also need to recognize how these strengths could be chink in somebody's armor, and how your weaknesses could be strengths. By recognizing these elements of your strengths and weaknesses, you can move to take action. This action will involve the improvement of your skills and abilities.

We are often preconditioned by influences surrounding our environment. Very few of us are mavericks, which are the nonconformists. These are the free spirited souls. Preconditions are a focus here in the "perspective-taking" development phase. This falls alone the theorization and unconditional ideas in regards to beliefs, thoughts, self, feelings, others, psychological states, and one's own continuation.

Leadership:
From Ability to Credibility

To develop businesslike skills and qualities one must learn to conform to standards of skills, competence, and characters that are commonly expected in a work environment. In order to move in this direction one must advance in the development phases.

Many people struggle to recognize the differences amid reality and unreality. This is because the use visualization as a form to produce fantasy-fiction thoughts, rather than non-fictional dreams. This is one of the predecessors that stand in the way of many people's success. One must learn to visualize self while staying in the real world and accepting that the world is both good and bad.

Theorization plays into perspectives. By applying theorization rules one can understand, listen better, and perform mental and physical activities whereas that entity is consciously aware of his or her behaviors. We can use our observation skills to advance any skill we possess.

CHAPTER 10

Observations and Growth

Observation in Self-Insight and Professional Growth

Observational learning has proven to be one of the sufficient strategic techniques that will help anyone improve their skills and advance toward professional growth. To improve this skill however, you must work through the self-concept stage, theorization, and the perspective training. According to experts, the observational learner often develops skills quicker than those that study from textbooks.

It is a proven fact that what you see is more accurate than most of what you hear. Thus, when one uses observational learning it often makes it difficult to refute any questions. Still, some all people see things differently, so this affects one's observational learning abilities. You can change this pattern however. All it takes is your willingness to continue learning. When you learn and gather facts and evidence, it makes it easier to develop an honest platform, which is one quality of a professional.

Learning is a gift. This is something we need

Leadership:
From Ability to Credibility

to continue doing all through our life; otherwise, the brain becomes inactive and starts to degenerate faster. By reading, writing and doing some puzzles you can increase your brain's ability to retain information, as well as improve your chance of living longer.

Observational learning is improved when you change the way you feel about life, and when you find facts to reform your misconceptions. Thus, the misconstruction of our understanding must be reformed in order to correct any way of misgiving behaviors and thinking patterns. You can use information online, go to the library, or better yet, enroll in college to retrain your mind. This will help you build on professional growth. Your image of you will seem better, as your skills, way of thinking, behaviors, etc all improve.

You can read books, articles, magazines or other materials to find more information on observational learning. The tactic has proven useful for many over the years. Even people with psychiatric disorders have gone a long way by using this natural gift. Visiting the Library or the Internet will put you in connection with several of the latest publications and articles listed online. Recently, the new book written on professional growth is available as well. You will find loads of information via the Internet, so start your search today. The sooner you get started, the quicker you will get going on professional growth.

Pay attention when you watch someone and observe your surroundings. Reflect on what you learn. This is one of the ways you can build your observational skills. Making observational learning a ritual will improve your skills. However, you should also participate in continuous learning so that you clear up any misconceptions that developed throughout your lifetime of learning.

Those that continue learning often live with a free mind. Their mind is not cluttered and rarely does anything get in the way of their professional growth. Many experts in psychology and in science often use observational learning to study human behaviors. They have learned much by using these applications in the field of scientific studies.

Each day if you practice observing and looking inward as well, followed by examining what you learn you can improve your skills: once you develop skills then you can take the next step in working toward professional growth. Use some of the natural practices, such as meditation to advance. This is one of the best practices that many people have used to help them improve all their skills, including focus, observation, and so on. You can also develop a higher plane of consciousness through this practice. Make it a habit and practice every day. This will ensure you get on the road to professional development. Start building your confidence.

Leadership:
From Ability to Credibility

Building Confidence

At the bottom of emotional starting place over and over again causes people to produce constructive or unenthusiastic thoughts. Over the course of one's life, they must take the road to unconscious, conscious, and subconscious learning to figure it all out. In the mind, we have channels that enable us to improve our professional, personal, performance, and other skills. We have the root of knowledge from our learning, experiences and events that we can draw from to advance toward professional growth.

One's way of thinking when optimistic can help that one to institute self-belief, which allows this one to build on the confidence through practice. Constructive social communication and self-help methods can help one to establish a new way of thinking. Our discernment and commencement reflect on the self and others. Often we must reprogram the mind to reframe our way of thinking. It is up to each of us to take action to adapt our way of thinking.

The world is a big place and offers many rewards, so why not step into self-insight, and advance toward professional growth. This is the start of building confidence and self-esteem.

We all have propensity and parallel individuality.

Each of us seeks appreciation, admiration,

love, and other constructive enforcer to make one stronger. We all must feel engrossed in something and fit into place. The common denominators say to us that all of us have the ability to use self-insight to advance toward professional growth. We all need encouraging influences in order to make it over the hurdle of self-development. The problem however is that many individuals panic at the thought of change. Change however is something that helps us to grow. Change is advancement and gives us prospective ways to improve our skills and abilities. Change enables one to adapt and make de rigueur or obligatory adjustments.

We need to develop an understanding in order to keep a clear mind. We need this clear mind to decide how we should respond or react to any situation, be part of the cause, verbalize, or generate a working natural environment. Change drives one to acknowledgment. This makes the entity feel the need to be in the right place, feel a sense of acknowledgment, and so on. Revolutionize changes can help build self-confidence and inspiration. All of us must institute a self-reliance to develop self-confidence. By paving the passageway to your advancement, you will exert the self harder, working on the way to building self-confidence and a winning way of thinking. We must pay attention to constructive feedback, since it helps us to adapt to making changes that drive us to professional growth alley.

We need to put emphasis on our progress while

Leadership:
From Ability to Credibility

seeing things in a broad spectrum. By checking one's internal and external advancements and growth, one can recognize his abilities and give rewards for the progress you have completed. We must stay focused. Focusing on one's competency and professional skills will help you to keep growing. We must fundamentally thrive to focus on the positive, and let the negative go. We can place great emphasis on accomplishment, motivation, management, performance, and other skills. We are obligated to recognize that our constructiveness is the way to encourage the self by reflecting on one's introspective, self-evaluation and correction progress. To learn more about developing a positive attitude for self-insight and professional growth, visit the Internet today. You will find loads of valuable information posted online. Look along the new age arena to find the latest techniques that have been helping people through professional growth for years. Start the decoding process today.

Decoding

People with privileged information, psychologists, and other professionals more often than not delineate or associate professional growth with a positive attitude. Various Internet areas online are looking more into ways to assist people with advancing their professional skills because of the new outsourcing changes. Online you will find a variety of theoretical quotes, instruction manuals, and abstract studies that make reference to the benefits of building a positive attitude to advance to professional growth.

We must stay focused and develop self-confidence in order to survive this crazy world. People that build up positive attitudes stay focused and looks for a better tomorrow. Instead of being part of the problem, they often become part of the solution. Some of the unconstructive or neutral minded however, strive harder to become part of the solution. We must focus on our conceptions and perceptions in order to adjust the way we think. We must also consider the environmental and social elements to adapt to a new way of thinking.

Social and environmental influences affect the way we think. These interactive influences also affect how one perceives life. We see the affects of social and environmental influences reflecting in our thoughts and behaviors. Our interaction abilities affect our entire life. This is only if we allow it. We need to consider the many factors including the way we see the world when it comes to advancing in expert growth.

Our measurement of thinking is often amid constructive, unconstructive and the in the intervening time. A number of people go beyond the boundaries of negative thinking that it pushes them to develop self-defeating habits. Each of us think depressing thoughts at times, yet at times, we have the measure of equilibrium. The pessimistic and positive thoughts can either, work

Leadership:
From Ability to Credibility

for us or against us. Unconstructive attitudes often cause one to feel despondent. One can feel disheartened, gloomy, and infuriated or preoccupied from thinking good thoughts. We know that when these feelings develop, something is amiss. At this time, one must find ways to seek answers to help that one fulfill his or her needs.

Unconstructive thinking changes our views, understanding, and way of thinking, value, and ethics. It twists one's entire life around. The manipulative tactics that take place around us affect our way of seeing things and can adjust our entire attitude. Professionals in the psychology sector, as well as the behaviorists typically delineate pessimistic thinking as an act that causes affects and reflects in our behavior and form as habits. The unconstructive changes derive from misconceptions and stem from the channels of knowledge, comprehension, and cognition. Cognition is one's ability to acquire knowledge through intuition, reasoning, and perceptions. Our physical functions discharge from the temperament of one's need to survive.

This survivalist need show a relationship with the human natural feeling. It is urbanized, and expanded through knowledge, experiences, and the proceedings of our precedent years of one's life. The responses often cause one to build up a collection of prototypes of behaviors in which it becomes perceptible in a collaborating ecosystem.

One's predilection or first choice reflects on our way of thinking. Our choices give a hand to enable us to manage our life on a survivalist scale. We have the power to self-examine our dislikes and likes through intensifying our first choice. Spoken objective collective with self-analysis through observational learning can benefit us by helping one to advance in professional growth. Visit the Internet today to find more ways to take action and advance toward professional growth, since each day is essentially changing the pace and the way in which the world can see things. Technology is advancing, which is making it necessary and essential to arrive at professional development.

Development

All of us have the power to make changes in the way we think, feel, or conduct our self. We can consider our level of development, knowledge, experiences, and the proceedings from the precedent years. We must practice natural techniques, which can help us to stay focused. Once preparation starts, we must weigh the difference amid unconstructive and positive. Rumination is the processes of thinking deeply on a subject. This course of action moves one through the process of discovery and developing original ideas.

Human expansion experts often have the same opinion that if one focuses on developing healthy self-esteem and virtuous quantity of self-belief that entity can prevail over the unhelpful

Leadership:
From Ability to Credibility

acts, feelings, behaviors, and so forth. A measure of the solution involves the interaction with encouraging influences. These influences will help you find a way to perceive things differently and often will activate your spirits with a few friendly words that come from well-rounded knowledge, contented moods, pleasant appearance, trustworthiness, and so forth.

How one contributes to information in some measure influence what mind-set we develop. Being around negative people all the time will only hold you back from professional growth. When you step into this growth arena, you want to arm yourself with the best breastplate that life can provide. This will ensure that you meet the expectations all the way through this growth phase. You must remove any negativity in your life to advance toward professional growth. Below is a list of negative that you can work on: Be sure to take action as soon as possible so that you become the pro that you long to be.

- Racism – the variants of racism only lead you to intolerance and bigotry. Do not be listed in this category, otherwise, you will not succeed in the business world.

- Hate – if you are filled with hate, revulsions, you are someone disgusting to others. Abandon hate and people will like you.

- Dishonest – if you are dishonest, people will

not trust you. Mendacious people often commit fraud or other crimes, simply because they set themselves up for the fall.

-        Disloyal – disloyal people are unfaithful, false, or fake, treacherous, and untrustworthy. Do not be a fictional character in someone's book rather develop faithful traits.

-        Doubt – When you have doubts, you will often hesitate when it is your turn to make a decision. If you are indecisive, people will consider you mistrusting, will feel suspicious of you, skeptic to listen, reserved, and so on. Do not be a smidgen. Rather become a lifelong learner, and adjust your way of thinking by finding the facts.

There are many other negative thinking habits you should consider. You should also consider your behaviors and habits. If you have unconstructive habits or behaviors, they often lead you straight down the road to damnation. You want to avoid hitting this road, since no benefits are offered. The only true outcome is self-defeat, self-destruction, and self-annihilation. Understand that you can extract from negative to produce positive. By develop a winning sense of humor you will start to see things in many ways, rather in a negative way. Learn to laugh and be cheerful. Everyone enjoys a person full of life. Imagine yourself sitting in a big, overstuffed leather office chair with a big fat expensive cigar in your hand. Often the relaxed people make it to the higher office grounds. You

Leadership:
From Ability to Credibility

can change in many ways, but try to keep it on a real note and on a constructive level so that you can improve your overall quality of life. Dismiss those negative thought.

Mark Zupo

CHAPTER 11

Learning Professionalism

Learning and Professional Growth

How the memory functions play into professional growth: We can learn from self-insight and professional growth by understanding the memory and how it retains information. The memory is a structure of membranes seated on short-term and long-term memory stems that stretch to the conscious, subconscious, and unconscious mind. One might ask, about the perimeter or maximum value of short-term memory when measured up to long-term memory. How does the short and long-term memory affect our inclusive realization? One might ask if the preservation of information cognizant or semi-conscious?

Understanding short and long-term memory:

Short-term is merely a transitory storage space where information is stored for a very short time. Short-term memory affects our cognizant, since if one wanted to summon up something that did not make it to the long-term memory, then that entity would apply great effort to bring to mind the details. In order to call to mind information from the short-term district of the brain you must act without delay.

Leadership:
From Ability to Credibility

The Long-term memory in contrast, is parts of our memory that retains information from our experiences whereas the information is permanent. The underpinning sources in the mind, such as the subconscious and unconscious mind catches bits and pieces where this part of the information is stored. In spite of everything we learn, all this information we congregate from nativity on, streams through the conscious, subconscious and unconscious mind whereas bits and pieces stay in the subliminal and unconscious area of the mind.

How information is retained:

The preservation of information is mutually cognizant and semi-conscious. This is because continuation of information channels down to the conscious, subconscious, and the cataleptic mind. For example, if you watch a television advertisement, likely you will retain information from the imagery or faces, but you may not call to mind the details, because you were not altogether focused, and the information channeled down to the subconscious region of the brain. You would have to scrutinize into this district to find out what you learned, or retained.

How understanding the mind benefits you:

By understanding the mind, and how the memory works, you can improve professional skills, since it will help you to appreciate, accept, and then find ways to meet your goal. Sometimes we must select our intelligence to move forward and find ways to meet our goals. Gardner left the best impressions when he drew attention to multiple, intelligence. According to Gardner, we have the power to use all of this intelligence, which include the musical intelligence, bodily and kinesthetic, spatial, linguistic, verbal, logical, mathematical, interpersonal, and intrapersonal.

Gardner explained to us that we could isolate the neuro-psychological aspects of our intelligence. Gardner believes that we have multi-intelligence because the body is a multi-neural component. These modules produce expressions, which represent how we memorize something, or execute rules and procedures. Read more about the levels of intelligence we posses. This will help you find ways to use all these levels to work toward professional growth.

Uses our seven levels of intelligence we can ultimately reach a higher plane of growth. The key is to integrate this intelligence and then bring them to work in unison. Harmonization is the major key points in understanding how to manage or operate a business. When there is no harmony, there is no peace. We recommend that you learn more about memory development, since it will help you with using your insight to advance toward professional growth. Insight takes us just around the corner to professional growth. We start to approach and reach the finish line when we use self-insight. Spend your life working toward self-growth.

Leadership:
From Ability to Credibility

Spending Time

Professional growth is one of the processes of self-development. We must spend a lifetime going through the changes that help us to develop professional skills. Sometimes life gets us down, but if we continue thriving ahead, often we reap many benefits.

Taking on the challenges that life tosses our way is the key to manipulate through this growing phase. You must continue to work through the stages throughout your life in order to keep advancing and pushing ahead. With each new change in our workplace and ecosystem, we must work meticulously today to accomplish our goals. We need to continuously learn, and do everything in your power to make it to the goal line.

Life takes us through many twists and turns, which sometimes make it difficult to focus and continue pushing to advance skills. Instead of life getting you down, get ahead of life by learning to accept change. Change is part of growing up. When we lose focus, it makes it demanding to deal with life, not to mention managing our duties at our workplace. Focus on what you must do to accomplish your goals. This is a major part of getting ahead. When you are aware and can find the ways to reform your behaviors.

Throughout the years, we generate a set of

attitudes, which involve our actions, beliefs, thoughts, and learned behaviors. This all keys a state of mind. By staying focused on professional growth and developing the mind, you can win the race. Understand that we must move to a higher consciousness in order to take control of our life and maintain this position. Our thoughts and memory enclose the consciousness, accomplishment and bring into being our feelings, thinking, perceptions, dreams, etc, and then supplies this information in a protected constituency to form as knowledge and memories. The level of thinking capacity is what determines our direction in life.

    You want to develop your creative and critical thinking abilities. This is creating a constructive mind in which you can form patterns or techniques to usher on toward professional growth by using your self-insight. The key is to get the mind and body to work in unison so that the two will labor with you. We can make the progress of professional growth smooth by retraining your actions and thoughts. You can question yourself to discover what you have learned. Use your self-talk and meditation skills to question the self. Reflect on what you learn. These are only a few ways to get on the road to professional growth.

    Making improvements is easy when you develop a drive and need to better the self. Many

Leadership:
From Ability to Credibility

experts tend to develop positive-thinking routine, a higher intensity of consciousness, self-insight and so on to take control of their life. The expert will take control of his or her thinking, behaviors, and perspective on life. Those with professional skills tend to build self- confidence through self-talk. Consistent reflection as well as many other techniques assists them with cultivating skills, such as self-control.

You will spend your life making changes, but with each step you take you will come one-step closer than the next person in professional growth. Many people lack this skill, which is causing growing concerns. In fact, many businesses now are requiring that people take on the responsibility of developing their professional mask. A mask they must continue wearing and consistently bettering each day. To learn more about professional growth visits the World Wide Web and read some of the latest articles. Reading will also improve your skills and take you closer to professional growth. Check the hierarchy of advancement.

Hierarchy

Maslow made some great points when he commented on the "hierarchy of needs." As stated by his viewpoint led him to believe that needs follow a formation, which all plays into professional growth. This structure involved a "lower level needs" that started with the fundamental continued existence that must be satisfied "before higher level needs guide a person's behavior." One of the highest levels is the need for "self-actualization."

After a short time ago, I began my journey writing about self-actualization, which is the flourishing personal development that necessitate for one to employ personal skills and abilities to attain and maintain professional attitudes. Personally, I can say that one must exercise meditation, yoga, self-talk, and other instinctive techniques to accomplish this level of realization.

In the workplace, many people have higher levels of needs that commence with basic survival skills. Other people are on the lower need scale. The ones on this scale tend to have inner guides that direct them toward professional growth. We see that the individuals that have higher needs are channeled down the right course while the lower level needs are not. With this in mind, we can see that someone could without problems form predisposed opinions of another, and make obvious their stereotype behaviors that interject a work environment. To some of us, labeling or categorizing others is one of the largest problems we all have to deal with, and shape the way one thinks, which is brought out in the open in their behaviors each day.

An additional drawback in the workplace is pointed out in various periodicals that speak of

Leadership:
From Ability to Credibility

favoritism. Preferential treatment in the work environment has repeatedly caused many issues that decline the count of professionalism. Employers and employees have a duty to show fairness to one another. Each of us has the responsibility to treat each other equal. This is an EEOC fair opportunity act in progress. The many consequences one will face for not illustrating EEOC characteristics and by ignoring the policies and procedures, thus the consequences should be the same for all. Bosses must treat employees equal; otherwise, it could cause conflict in the work environment. People often develop hostile attitudes when they are not treated justly. With so much competition in the world, as well as the low morale issues, lack of respect, etc, it is hard on all of us, which is why equal fairness should be demonstrated each day.

We all must develop professional behaviors, thinking, and so on to rebuild skills that were torn away by the entire negative that takes place in our world. We must reform our thinking and behaviors while staying clear of negative people.

Despite that, these rules exists many employees, employers, and even the law ignores these rules. Mary also tells us "In the work environment, the supervisor, owners, or managers are responsible for motivation. The morale on the job will determine the success, attitude, and dedication of the employees.

Mark Zupo

Being positive, honest, and treating employees with respect will create a positive work environment with working and willing employees. Introducing new ideas, teamwork including supervisors participating, rewards, understanding personal, and business issues will motivate staff to meet deadlines, be attendance conscious, and adhere to policies and procedures. A motivating supervisor with a positive attitude will gain the respect of the employees and the willingness for their contribution to be complete and concise."

You can find more information online. It only takes a few minutes to check out the Internet to find additional information to help you grow. Go Internet today!

Levels

Your about out of school what are you going to do with your life? This is where you need to really be thinking about who you want to become this is one a professional level. Let us get real have you really thought about as a child you would say I would like to be a doctor when I grow up or maybe even a police offers but that is a far, as it would go right. You would not look into yourself to discover what you would like to be right. Well it is time to do that in less you enjoy making your professional career working at a burger joint.

Let us take a long hard look at the world today

Leadership:
From Ability to Credibility

are you really going anywhere working at your local burger joint. More than likely not, do you like it I mean really like it, is this going to be something that you would like to do for the next forty years of your life. More than likely not right, well then get off the sofa and away from the T.V. and do something about it.

This is going to take some time but if you really would like to make something out of yourself so that your will be noticed in life then what is time nothing right. Therefore, what do you have to do to get this in order? The first thing you are going to have to do is to take along look inside your mind as well as your soul and be able to figure out what you would like to do with your life. You have to be able to realize that you really truly want this and then you will be on the road to a better life style coming your way. This better life style is going to come to you in less you really want this to happen it going to take some work and effort on your behave. However, I believe in you and I think if you put your mind to it, you can do anything that you want in life.

How do I get started in the new and professional me?

Once you have decided what you want to do with your life then it is all really easy to get there and do something about it. This may mean you have to be able to think all the time with a positive attitude this will have to go with you though out your lifetime. Not only while you are at work but also while you are at play. You will notice that once you are able to see thing with a positive attitude you will notice how well things will be going for you. You will be able to see things in a better way you will notice that you will be able to look at yourself in a different way this is all to help you out.

If then and when you are ready, that is when you make the big move to see how to get what you really want to do. This could mean that you have to go to school to better your education or take some kind of training who knows whatever it may be then go for it and do not stop until you get there. We have all had to do something in our life to better it so this is not going to be too hard we have all lived though it and made it. You will be just fine on the road to successful side of you.

Differences

Today in the real world, we all have to work doing something or the other to make it work for us. So how do we do this well we have to learn to reprogram our self but first we have to be able to want it not for just the work field but for our self as well. This is going to take some work and affect but again if you want it you will make it. Today world is not going to good, as we all know this. We are going to have to make it somehow to make it happen this is going to be up to you and how fast you get it.

Leadership:
From Ability to Credibility

The world today is not going to get any better so in order to make some improvements we have to do something for us, in order to get anywhere. If we do not then we are going to go nowhere fast. We have to try to make some improvement on our end so that we have or at least try to get a better life for us and our family. Our families are very importing to us we they are suppose to be any ways so why not work together to make something happen.

What do I have to be able to do to be able to changes my ways of thinking?

You do not have to do much of anything to be able to change your ways of thinking but you do have to want the change for you. No one can make just changes for you; you are going to have to want them to help to improve you and your life style. Once you have done this you will feel a lot better about yourself and others around you will also be able to tell the difference

What is the first thing that I have to do in order to start changing?

The first thing that you should do is make sure this is want you want. Once you have done that you need to learn to be able to think with a positive attitude this will help you to be able to make the right decisions once you have done this things will come to you more clearly. It makes you capable of making all the right calls.

Once this is done then you are going to have to be able to decide what you want to do with your life as a professional this means making the right choices in choosing the right career that you want. This is something again that you're going to have to be able to look deep in yourself to be able to decided what you want to do as a career woman or man. This is going to take some time doing so do make the decision over night take some time with it for this is supposed to be a long time career so take some time not a lot of time but some. This will help you to be able to decide what you want to become in your life.

Once this is done then you are going to have to go and get started getting ready for your in professional in life. This may include going back to school so that would be the first place that I would go for answer. If they are not able to help you, they will be able to lead you on the right path to your profession that you want to become in your life. This is a big step. Yet, if you want something, you will go out and get it. If you want something bad, enough it will happen you as a person will make it happen for you.

Schooling

Have you ever took time to think as a child what you would like to be we have all been there and for the most of us what we thought back then isn't want we are today or what we want to be. We all

Leadership:
From Ability to Credibility

have dreams of being rich one day. Nevertheless, have you really thought about how you were going to get to where you want to be? It is going to take some work getting there as well as the able to go the career you want to become. Some of us are going to have to work at this and others it will come natural to them. We have to be taught how to make the right discussion in order to get what we want in life so here am going to talk to you about getting just what you want and how to be able to get that professional that you want in life.

How do you pick what you want to do as a professional?

When you are trying to pick your life long career there are some things that you are going to have to do. The main thing that you are going to have to do is sit down and think about what you are good at. This means things like working with people, or working in a factor, or whatever you like to do. When you are trying to pick a career this is supposed to be the job that you are going to stay with. Although this does not always happen that way but that is the main idea for getting a career. Then after you have done that, you are going to have to figure what it is going to take for you to get there and get it done. With most professional careers you have to go to college to get some kind of degree, in which this is not going to hurt anyone, you are never too old to go to school. Although there are many people that think otherwise and that is why most of them are working flipping burgers in a local burger joint. Do not get me wrong now days you can make money doing that but is it really what you want to do for the rest of your working days. If so then go for it and have fun if not then it is not too late to do something about it.

The steps to becoming something that you want is not hard to do but you have to know first what kind of study you enjoy. You want to become a nurse or do you feel like you want to become a teacher. Once you have an idea, you call your local college and they will walk you through it. You will notice that you will feel a lot better if you decided to do this. Why is that well your attitude will change greatly, you will feel a lot better about yourself. You will be able to walk with your head up high. Just think that if you are doing this in the younger years in your life you will be able to show your children what to do for them to become all they can be, if you are doing this in the later years that are ok to your making a great example for your grandchildren. It is always a good thing to want to learn we learn something every day in our life learn is a lifelong skill. We will always learn we may not that we are learning but we are learning something new every day of our life.

Leadership:
From Ability to Credibility

Education

What we have to do to get what we want in life?

In order to get what you want in life you are going to have to work at it. It is not going to come to you on a silver plate. Most of us want things in life that it is almost impossible to have, without some kind of schooling you are not going to get there your just not. We go though school until we are eighteen years old then they are telling us that we have to go back to school to make something with our self we are thinking this isn't fair to us but it all good we can make it.

We are going to have to work at it but it will come with some hard work and the ability to become what we want we can make our dreams come true. No matter what we do in life, we have to be able to have a good outlook on life as well as be able to do something to help us to better our self.

Now days there isn't much work out there in our work fields so getting an good job and being able to keep it is going to be a task for some of us. Just take a look at it the one that are hiring you are going to look at your school as well as we work history. If you are headstrong, and feel you do not need to continue learning, or that you do not need a good work history to get your dream job, then you are off to a bad start. When it comes someone that has went to school all their life and has a great work history they just want to upgrade their career which one do you think is going to get the job your right the one that is showing some efforts. Not the one that doesn't care about anything in life and thinks it going to come to them on a plate it not going to happen when you want to become a professional you're going to have to make it happen.

How do you make this happen?

In order to make this dream come true you are going to have to have better outlook on life. The first thing you are going to have to change is your attitude on the way your thinking that you do not need all of this cheap to make something out of yourself because you do need this cheap. The cheap way out is not the right way out. If you are taking this road, then you are on the way to self-defeat. We all have to work toward something in order to get something good in return so why not start now while you are young enough to do something about your ways of thinking. You have to be able to think better in may have to do with your attitude I do not know but you have to be able to think with a positives side. If you are wanting to really change then this is not going to be hard for you if you are not your going to have to work at it. You will notice that if you want the change then it will come to you easier than if you do not want to change then it going to be hard for you to make that professional sideshow. However, once you have did want it takes to change then you will be able to enjoy life to the

Leadership:
From Ability to Credibility

fullest that you can. It can and will happen if you want it bad enough. All you have to do is to apply yourself and reprogram your mind that you want to change and go for it.

Probing

There are so many ways to get what you want these days there is no reason for you not to be able to get that profession that you are wanting. It may take some time but it ok that is all we have is time if you think about it that is the truth there is nothing but time in our world. Instead of thinking that you do not have much time, think about the time you will not have when you are working 70 hours a week just to make ends meet.

Although we are working, we can spend some of the minutes centering in on our way to improve our skills. Without time we would not be anything. Have you taken a long deep look into your head to decide what you want to do when you really grow up? This is something they are suppose to get you to do when you are in school is to show you how to become a professional. Who want to think about school when we are young and we do not want to send all of our time in school?

Most of us are thinking at that time I do not need school to make something out of myself I will get a job. Most of us did that but if you are anything like others, soon you will find out that it was not what you really wanted to do for the rest of

Mark Zupo

my life. Sometimes gets you by but as you get older and had a family of your own and soon noticed that what you was doing was not going to get you the life you wanted for your children. We have to then think of how and what to do to improve our life so that we could set a good example for my children, this is when we have to take a long look in the mirror and think. You may have found out that you wanted to help sick children and adults so you decided that you were going to go back to school to become a nurse. That is what some people did; yet as they went back to school and become that nurse, they learnt later that this was not really want they wanted. Some people run into some hard times in getting their degree but if these people would stick with it, things would work out fine.

Now that I got it I look back at all the hard times that I have and I think to myself if I would of knew in my younger years but I would never of did anything different. It was a lot of hard work but I did it and that is all that matters not how hard it was but that I work and did something with my life even though I was older I still did something to make something with myself. So now, when my kids come home and say mom we are having career day at school I try to inspire my children to go and see what they offer them out there in the world today. I did not have that when I was in school.

Leadership:
From Ability to Credibility

Like they say I do not need school well they will soon see that they do need school. We cannot make our child do anything that they do not want to do, but we can try to show them the right way in life. Children learn what is good and bad, we cannot make their minds up for them, but we can teach them how to make the right ones in life to get what they want and desire though out there years. Start probing into your life.

CHAPTER 12

Breakthroughs in Professionalism

Breakthrough in Self-Insight and Professional Growth

We can make breakthroughs by looking inward at our own abilities. Self-insight is a working skill that helps us to develop new skills. We can look at our experiences, past, and knowledge to make our life better.
By probing, in the self one can exploit into this mind and make new breakthroughs, to develop new ideas, and to find solutions that will direct them on the way to professional growth. We all need to expand our skills.

From the time that we are born, we often think or at least we wander with the developments that are drifting in and out. We often think that this is the journey that lets us drift into the streams that confuses one. Many people stay insides these areas.

Why should you have to stay in a confined room when you are able to get out and see the world? You will then be able to notice that the world can offer you more than you think it can. If you are willing, it can offer you the biggest pot of gold that you will not even be able to use both hands to move it. Inside this pot of gold there is a river

Leadership:
From Ability to Credibility

flowing deep with the knowledge of processional growth.

The inside of our self has all the answer that we will need to be able to find that path the will lead us to find that professional growth that we are all looking for in life. All you will have to do is take a little trip inside that mind of yours and you will be able to find that inner self that you have been searching for. This will really amaze you and give you the information that will channel you and help you to reprogram your ways of thinking. This will send you on your way to the path of professional growth.

Once you have tapped in to all that you and have used up all of your fuel you will have to find another source to get fuel you tank back up to be able to move to the next day. We have to sometimes get into the source we do this by using meditation, self-emending or even when we go exploring. There are so many ways that you are able to get into your insights and be able to use then to help you to get to your professional growth. You as a person have to be willing to get there. This is going to take some time but can be done.

These will be some of best techniques that you will be able to see. You will want to set your goals so they will meet your purpose in life. This will give you something to look forward to and be able to keep you motivated enough to be able to reach your goals.

These goals should be set so that you are able to reach the businessperson in you. Some people will be able to do this and then again, there are some that will have to strive to reach what they want in life, this will also affect that professional growth line that they may want to use.

When you want to become a professional at something this will have to be a state of mind that you are in. If you want to see, what professionalism is then you are going to have to see and meet the standards and applying skills, and the character as expected by meeting highly trained people that work in this field every day, once you become a professional they look into the attire picture despising their own ways of life.

When you see a professional in a western atmosphere and they dress this way they are making their self fit it despite how they feel about what they have done. In addition, they way they are wanting to dress.

Discovering Options

We often do not take time to stop and think about our learning progress. Many people think that it is merely a procedure we all must endure. What makes us learn how to talk, think, or even recall the good things as well as the bad things is sometimes a mystery. As you can see, it is essential to explore options to find alternatives that

Leadership:
From Ability to Credibility

will lead you to success. We must explore to see what is available. Visit the Internet to open up new ways for professional growth today.

We have several options today that can help us advance. One of these options is continuous learning. With continuous learning, you want to be in a comfortable environment. You want to make sure that the setting is comfortable as possible. Make sure that your desk is at the right height. You might want to have some background music. Burn some aroma scents to help you relax. Try listening to the new natural sound CDs to help you relax. Once you have, done all of the things you are ready to move to the next step. Besides continuous learning, you have other alternatives as well.

Learning is a fun part of life. Continue learning and you will do well in all things that you do. Enjoy life now, since there are not any promises of tomorrow. Take some time to explore the inner depths of your mind to learn more about your insights.

Discovering through mental exploration:

Mental exploring is the process of learning from using our memory. Our memory permits us to store information, which channels down to various areas of the mind. When you want to use it, you have to go through it and do some filing in a sense of speaking. By using your memory tool, you can remember ever thing in your file cabinet good and bad, the good is easier for you to remember. However, you want to expose the bad to abandon the emotions that emerge from your pain. Bad things are most of the time blocked from your mind. This is for the reason you do not want to think of all the pain that it caused you so you just do not use it as much only if you have to, which only holds you back.

We all must learn to relax. You have to use these procedures as well as using other methods. People need to relax in order to get some relief from things that stress them. When you learn to relax, you will be able to learn to deal with your stress better.

Some of the reason we are so stressed is because we may not know how to use methods to learn to relax. Therefore, we block everything that we have learned in the past that hinders us from relaxing. The problem is obvious, which is most times people do not want to learn something new that could perhaps help them grow by relaxing.

There are many ways to relax your mind. We have to learn to file our thoughts in the right place in our filing cabinet. In which most of us forget how to do that. Relaxation will encourage you to find ways to work toward professional growth.

The quandary makes it harder to think clearly. For that reason, successfully to build awareness and to develop your skills you must face our past and find the answers that wait inside of you. Take some

Leadership:
From Ability to Credibility

time to explore the Internet today and find some more good news waiting for you at the websites online.

Selecting Self-Insight and Professional Growth

The fact is we all must use the ability to be reasonable; on the other hand, in many districts of understanding human behaviors, we must climb over the limitations of commonsense grounds. We must build up elevated levels by on the increase new insights. This engrosses creating a higher plane of conscious consciousness by reaching out to inspect the differentiation and correspondence accompanied by others and ourselves. In view of the fact, that, many problems are many-sided; we must look deeper and prolong and look for answers to give explanation to human behaviors, which precisely why it correlates to professional growth.

Professional growth in terms is the development of studying the human mind and how it works by using scientific applications. The characteristics of mental composition and the personality, as well as the associated behaviors is part of this study, which is conducted in groups or individual settings that exhibit these people to analyze through observation, how they engage in a given activity. We see that work issues associate deeply with psychological aspects, as well as professional growth, simply because it is the mind and its thoughts, feelings, and so on that stream from the emotions – coming from the unconscious, subconscious, and conscious mind; in this way, the actions are often urbanized from unconscious thoughts that biologically take place each day. This is without a doubt psychology associated.

MISCONCEPTIONS are the leading cause for why the human race all face the many problems we do today. The only probable solution for solving these issues is to promote continuous learning – subconscious learning, and then move to take other actions to reorganization the misconceptions. These misconceptions then reach your destination from past – learning, knowledge, experiences, surveillance, and proceedings.

Stereotyping is a major problem in the work place and is not a qualified professional skills or quality. This is an oversimplified perception, homogeneous image of groups or individual that has many twisted views – It is the development of plummeting someone to oversimplified categories – Compare to the standard dictionary – Bias – Preconceived notion, preconceptions – unfairness.

We must find ways to reshape our mind and dust off the residue of built up misconceptions that come into our life from external influences.

Imagine yourself sitting down at a conference table with a personification of your insecurity sitting in front of you. Face it evenly and do not shirk. Plan on what to do about it and do it without a second thought. After you have acknowledged and

Leadership:
From Ability to Credibility

accepted your insecurity, it is time to face it head-on. Charge like a prized bull charging a matador. Picture your insecurity as that gaudily dressed man teasing you with his red rag. Charge with your newfound horns like there's no tomorrow.

If you are afraid of people, get a job in a trade, which makes it inevitable for you to meet and talk with people. If you feel insecure about the way you look, dress up and take a stroll at the mall or the park.

Take it one-step at a time and reward yourself for every little thing you achieve. Never get frustrated if in case it is not going as fast as you wish. Relax. Take a deep breath. See a movie. It will not do you harm to take one small step at a time – nobody ever said it would be a cakewalk.

Rebuilding your self-esteem will be very trying and taxing but is essential for a more effective consciousness and self-development. Keep in mind, if you are able to do it, the most that would benefit from this improvement is no one else but you.

Skilled Self-Insight and Professional Growth

A level of competency is necessary to enforce that one succeeds. Competency is built on experience and knowledge. By gathering information, you can build on knowledge by finding the facts. Gathering information will, in time build skill, realization, and wisdom.

Mark Zupo

Professionalism is becoming one of the major requirements for employees and employers in the business world. Because of the many problems, businesses are placing greater emphasis on education and learning. Some of the changes in business have lead to major changes and expectations. Businesses are supposed to be a place where people exchange ideas without conflicts. Many of the conflicts that take place in the businesses and real world are due to lack of professionalism. The world is moving rapidly toward Internet business whereas many companies are selling products, services, and so forth online. E-mails are being sent each day, which has posed issues. Many businesses are expecting employees to write professional electronic mails to promote their services or products. The problem with this is that the employee must learn proper marketing strategies, writing, and other skilled tasks to ensure that the connections are meet without complications. Internet providers will bar those that send emails in spam form, so company employees must learn to prevent, act, and respond to emails without violating the Internet providers' rules and policies.

Leadership:
From Ability to Credibility

PART 2:

Leadership

*Excerpt from the 2009 Interview and conversation with Speaker / Author and Thought-Leader Mark Zupo

Leadership Potential

Practices of Exemplary Leadership

Modeling the Way

One finds leadership in predictable places and develops personal leadership styles from experiences and opportunity. A person who qualifies as a leader will exhibit the leadership qualities and competencies that are fundamental to driving extraordinary actions that get things done in organizations. There have been many opportunities of this in my life that might be highlighted as examples of leadership forming experiences. They are defined as the opportunities that teach through experience and opportunities are not left to chance or prediction. Talent for leadership cannot be taught unless one experiences the nuance of opportunity for involvement with others under many different circumstances. (Palmer 2001).

As a young man, my destiny would be focused

on achievement and success. The catalyst for these qualities was the recognition that I could be more, have more, experience more than what was readily visible. Some realization was the result of providence as much as opportunity. The influence of three people helped to shape my future desires and path to success as a leader. The unifying message from each was honor, respect, credibility and humility. Each was a model for my successes.

In Practice

The model for success, my mentors, knowingly or unknowingly, offered the opportunity to develop self-awareness for my right to achievement based on my ability to work for it. Work ethic became the mainstay for my actions as a young man in a big world. Leading by example, they modeled the way for my success with illustrations of personal actions that lay the groundwork for my ability to act similarly when presented with similar opportunities.

In such actions, my mentors made use of empowerment as the vehicle for my learning in a manner that made their example personal and a delivered value of ownership. This practice of empowerment allows for accountability as well as responsibility.

An example of the second practice in this model of exemplary leadership is inspiration. I have been

Leadership:
From Ability to Credibility

fortunate to have great inspiration during the formative years of (me) my growth as a leader. They include the opportunity of chance encounter and unpredicted opportunity to be mentored by a few great people with a shared vision for achievement and success. It is important to recognize that it is often the unexpected and the unpredictable opportunities that offer the greatest opportunity for leadership growth. Leaders must embrace these!

The ultimate example of a shared vision came in the way of delegation of responsibilities that were the vehicle for success and failure for me. The shared vision aligned my willingness to experience the opportunity to reach goals that many men will never aspire to. They were aviation / aerospace related. The aviation and aerospace industry is ripe with opportunity to excel when the opportunity avails to explore danger and intrigue.

There, I found many challenges if I were to become recognized as an authority in the industry. Those challenges required much study, huge effort to maintain a standard of excellence and the willingness to share my experiences with those coming after me. The vision included the responsibility to mentor others. The challenge was to develop my credibility and authority to add value to my ability to mentor others.

Mark Zupo

The vision among aviation enthusiasts is one of glamour and excitement beyond the everyday. This came when I was opportune to the experience of space travel vicariously through Astronaut John Glenn.

The Challenge

The greatest challenge for a leader, whether established or fledgling, is to state the mission in a clear and concise manner so to be understood and to establish their authority founded by credibility. In aviation, there is no example of a rise to the top without "paying one's dues" in the process. Training is imperative to the mission, a mission is imperative to the purpose and purpose is imperative to the success. Without these interrelated scenarios, success is unlikely and achievement more accidental than accurate.

I have spent many hours, almost ten-thousand to be exact, flying missions safely and accurately as a result of exacting mentoring and specific mission-focused training. Only when the opportunity reveals itself during a critical decision-making moment will one challenge the standard operating procedure and waiver from the norm. This can challenge the process and determine life-changing opportunity

Leadership:
From Ability to Credibility

and an experience one will not soon forget. This is when the mentoring and training will be revealed in precise and almost involuntary actions that determine your future and the future of your associates, coworkers or students. (Kouzes 2008).This is a great example!

The next leadership practice is enablement. I am fortunate that in my experience as an aviator, enablement is a crucial factor in the procedure for developing leadership qualities. In training, empowerment is the foundation for accountability and responsibility as a pilot and flight instructor. This must be demonstrated to accept the responsibility of property and life. In the aviation standard for training the term is "crew resource management". This is the ultimate example of empowerment as demonstrated when the complete responsibility for airplane and passengers, mission and safety. Awkward.

As training is the most important factor in carrying out any safe aviation operation, currency is parallel in importance and weigh heavily as the enabler to the mission. Currency is the fluency and practiced abilities one has in the enabled environment as a crewmember regardless of the founding principle or status of the flight, commercial operations or general operations. My first opportunity of empowerment and enablement came on a routine training mission in the civilian environment. During a training flight in a small twin aircraft in which I was to achieve a commercial multi-engine certificate rating, we approached an airport in Alabama with all of the confidence any trained and experienced pilot could expect. The normal approach was unremarkable until the cabin was permeated with the smell of fuel. We were to learn later that a critical valve just under the firewall ruptured in flight and allowed aviation fuel to leak into the cockpit.

As immediate as the circumstance revealed (its' self), the passenger I was carrying was an FAA designated examiner whose job was to evaluate my performance and was to be present for an example of the very reason for expert training and currency. He was there to test my abilities and today would be the real life test. The first reaction and standard operating procedure in this kind of circumstance was for the senior of the crewmembers to immediately assume command as the junior member facilitates their role in assessment, containment and communications. Respectively, communicating to air traffic control that we were facing sure death unless we landed immediately.

As crew resource management is the leader for an exacting and precise operation, empowerment is

Leadership:
From Ability to Credibility

the mother. My examiner, Mr. Clyde Shelton, saw the opportunity for the ultimate test of my abilities. He was to empower me to act as I had been trained and work with him in a collaborative manner to accomplish the task at hand, respectively, saving his life and mine. As the leader that I was trained to be, I immediately stated verbally, "My airplane". This was the verbal queue to the secondary officer, no matter their rank, to understand their role and commence with the operation just handed us. Mr. Shelton(,) nodded to me that he would assume the secondary role without saying a word and began the procedure of notifying air traffic control of our situation while simultaneously facilitating the checklist.

His ability to empower me, whether assumed or directed, was the vehicle for enablement. His job became the block for distractions and influences that might inhibit me to act with precise method to get us on the ground. Without the influence of exterior factors that might distract me like crying passengers or structural anomalies, I was able to land, bring the airplane to a stop, extract ourselves from the airplane and recover safely. The task accomplished with confidence, precision and the enablement that I had trained for many times. (Slaski 2003).
The power of enablement was realized in the moment that we looked at each other without

words, smiled and a nod.   This scenario emphasizes the importance of the leader having those skills and knowledge needed within his career field. Do you feel that effective leaders must be experts in their field?

   This was dramatic but real example of understanding between professionals, enablers, leaders. That is when I realized that my leadership abilities had not only been established but had been cemented through the vehicle of enablement.
   Notwithstanding emergent circumstance, aviation provides many opportunities to develop and exhibit qualities of leadership, empowerment and encouragement. State of mind and presence of mind are crucial factors in every flight becoming a success and build upon a pilot's ability to use their confidence as the vehicle for professionalism. Regardless of the structure of the environment, a pilot is also human requiring encouragement and support from other professionals in the industry.

   Flight requires the extreme planning for the safety of every mission. It is when planning fails that gives opportunity for failure in flight. It is a crucial step in a process whose chain must not be broken less calamity present itself. Empowerment without encouragement gives a hollow sense of control. (George & Sims 2007). This is revealed when a pilot is faced with a leadership decision

Leadership:
From Ability to Credibility

when flying as single pilot, which means flying alone no matter the mission or cargo.

An appropriate resource for every pilot, manager, administrator or leader involves encouragement. The encouragement support from peers or other professionals lays the foundation for one to believe in their training and ability to use what they have learned in practice. Without encouragement, confidence suffers and simple tasks have opportunity to fail. As a leader, there is little room to show weakness and a lack of confidence undermines one's credibility and authority. (Balkundi 2001).

The attraction one feels for their passion, like flying is to me, requires a level of competence and security. Encouragement can provide the confidence in self through the vehicle of empowerment. To believe that one can achieve anything that another man can or has is real and concrete by perception alone. (Whitman 2009). My ability as a Master Flight Instructor is tested when I encourage other pilots to become a flight instructor, but to achieve the highest level of status as Master Flight Instructor. The best the industry and training can produce.

Mark Zupo

To the point, it is in my encouragement to other professionals to achieve more, realize their abilities more and utilize their confidence to continue to improve.

Summation

Training one to be a leader is not enough; it requires the support of encouragement with the confidence found in training from those who have come before them as leaders. They become mentors as they realized their goals and offer encouragement to fledgling leaders whose experience is yet to be tested. I owe some of my success to a friend and mentor, Chuck Barton, who encouraged me to finish school if I were to realize my goals of commercial pilot and flight instructor.

Because of his encouragement, his recognition of my abilities and passion, understanding the need for support as a mentor, I was moved to follow through on my dream and accomplished a level of success most never find. The glamour and attraction of aviation's hold on those who aspire to find achievement and success can be found in the leadership qualities that encouragement delivers. If one believes he or she can then there is little to stop their achievement. (Leithwood 1992).

Leadership:
From Ability to Credibility

What I have learned from my life experiences is that I can, I have and I will achieve everything I aspire to with training and focus if I so desire. I understand the mechanisms that propel ordinary people to successes that others only dream of. Action is the vehicle and empowerment is the key that unlocks the power of encouragement. Henry Ford was quoted as saying, "If you think you can or you think you can't...you're right", and a simple yet powerful statement of one's ability to believe in themselves. I have come to believe that you can do anything if supported, empowered and encouraged to.

Q-1: Mark, How can anyone unleash their leadership potential?

"Here are the immediate actions you can take to start you on your leadership journey:

There is a steady flow of information in the form of books, articles, white papers and training all in the context of ["what is leadership" or "how to develop a leader"]? In this issue, I will talk about two others that I believe might be on the minds of a lot your readers and listeners. In addition, they are:

Why does better leadership make a difference? And

How does better leadership achieve those differences?

Mark Zupo

Leadership is a unique form of human behavior that requires the integration of character, knowledge and experience. So what can you do if you step up and unleash your leadership potential? Change the world.

Your journey to unleashing your leadership potential begins with a great understanding of self. Discover your personality traits and how they relate to leadership. When we know ourselves, we can maximize our positive traits, and become aware of our weaker areas, which help us to achieve our leadership potential. Once you understand and know yourself, next you must hone your communication skills.

These are not limited to your public speaking skills either. This includes your writing style and your body language. Your ability to communicate effectively enhances your ability to improve interpersonal relationships. Another important skill is to learn how to learn. Examine different teaching methods and learning styles to identify how you and those you may lead learn best. This skill will greatly enhance your ability to make decisions and give clear instructions.

An Exceptional Leader is one that recognizes the value of harnessing the skills and abilities of team members and leads them toward greater efficiency and effectiveness.

...And so leader is not a title and leadership is not something you are born into. Leadership is

Leadership:
From Ability to Credibility

something you develop.

Q-2: How does one know if they are a leader or a slacker?

"Do you claim to be a Leader in your business or your field of expertise? I have noticed that many people claim to be Leaders, but I consider them Slackers instead. A Slacker is someone that basically likes to give instruction or direction, but takes no action on advancing themselves or their business.

Do you claim to be a Leader in your business or your field of expertise?

I have noticed that many people claim to be Leaders, but I consider them Slackers instead. A Slacker is someone that basically likes to give instruction or direction, but takes no action on advancing themselves or their business.

Does this describe you; you are up-line or someone else on your Mastermind Team? Here are some clues that might help you out.

Leader: Praises his/her team and offers encouragement

Slacker: Quick to find fault and slow to give praise

Leader: Holds himself/herself to a higher standard that his/her team

Slacker: Has a high level of expectation for his/her

team but does not hold him/her to that same standard

Leader: Leads by example and is a role model for his/her team

Slacker: Blends in with crowd and never steps up to take a leadership role

Leader: Has deep-rooted belief in his/her business and leads new teammates through the growth process (learning the business and facing obstacles)

Slacker: Convinces a person to join his/her team then pawns them off on someone else or simply pushes them to the side (Referred to as "sign and drop")

Which of these characteristics, best describes you and your teammates? Be honest with yourself.

Just remember, that a leader must lead and nourish others through the growth process. If he/she loses integrity and fails to take action, then this same failure mindset will ripple down to his/her teammates. A team will duplicate their leader and their leader's actions.

Let me ask you one last time…Are you a Leader or a Slacker?"

Leadership:
From Ability to Credibility

Blueprint for Leadership - How to Be a Better Leader

Q-3: Mark, How can anyone be a better leader?

"Here is a description of what people want in a leader. How do you compare?

If you were to build a house, you would begin with a blueprint. This blueprint proves useful because it contains more than directions on how to build a house. It also describes the finished house.

So, what does this have to do with leadership?

Last month I asked an audience of leaders to tell me the characteristics of an ideal leader. Their answers were (in the order collected):

A good listener, enthusiasm, passion, shows appreciation, a visionary, role model, trusting, integrity, organized, knowledgeable, credibility, persuasive, charisma, team building, clarity of purpose, problem solver, attitude of service, leads by example, patience, willing to act without complete knowledge, understands followers, consistent, empowers other people, and adapts to change.

I will add that this is essentially the same list that I receive from other audiences when I ask this question. From this come some useful insights.

1) Notice what the list contains. All of these characteristics relate to the human side of leadership. That is interesting because I often hear people minimize this side of leadership with terms like "soft" or "touchy feely." Actually, applying these characteristics requires more strength than not.

2) Notice what the list excludes. Absent from this list (and all lists from other programs) are characteristics such as stern, mean, serious, short tempered, vindictive, tough, angry, harsh, punitive, controlling, violent, or ruthless. In addition, that is interesting because many popular representations of leadership emphasize at least one of these "hard" characteristics. In fact, these characteristics are the refuge of those who lack the strength (or the skills) to apply the human side of leadership.

3) How about you? How would you rate yourself as a leader compared to the list of positive characteristics? If you were to survey the people who report to you, how would they describe your leadership? Would they list characteristics from the "soft" list or from the "hard" list? Could you become more effective by improving upon any of the "soft" characteristics? In addition, how about the other leaders in your organization? Do they truly maximize human potential?

People want leaders who treat them with genuine compassion, courtesy, and respect. They want

Leadership:
From Ability to Credibility

leaders who help them become more successful. They want leaders who inspire them with a vision for a better world and show them how to go there."

Simple Leadership Basics

Q-4: Mark, What are the leadership basics we all look for to be successful leaders?

"A great cloud of jargon, debate, and junk theory surrounds the idea of leadership, what it is, who does it, and how to do it well. However, if you have just been promoted, and you are responsible for a group for the first time, there are only a few things you really need to know about leadership.

When you are promoted and become responsible for the performance of a group, you become a leader. However, you do not undergo some magical change. In fact, it will probably take you over a year just to get the basic understanding of your role requirements and responsibilities.

A great cloud of jargon, debate, and junk theory surrounds the idea of leadership, what it is, who does it, and how to do it well. However, if you have just been promoted, and you are responsible for a group for the first time, there are only a few things you really need to know about leadership.

When you are promoted and become responsible for the performance of a group, you become a leader. However, you do not undergo some magical change. In fact, it will probably take you over a year to completely adjust to your new role.

You are a leader because the people in your group treat you like one. The only choice you have is what kind of job you will do.

When you become a leader, your power actually goes down. As an individual contributor, you just have to decide to work harder, longer or smarter to improve performance. When you are responsible for the performance of a group, the group is your destiny. They choose whether to act or not.

When you become a leader, your influence goes up. The people who work for you pay attention to what you say and do. They adjust their behavior accordingly.

The result is that you use your behavior (what you say and do) to influence the behavior of the people who work for you to achieve a defined objective.

Achieving the objective is part of your job as a leader. The other part is caring for your people.

It may be possible to achieve good short-term results without caring for your people. Nevertheless, you cannot achieve long-term success for you or your company without the willing cooperation of the best folks you can find.

At the end of the day, you can measure your leadership based on those two standards. Did we accomplish the mission? Are the members of my

Leadership:
From Ability to Credibility

group better off today than yesterday?

You can find out more about all of this and learn it almost effortlessly from my High-Performance presentation,

Leadership: From ability to Credibility"

Train Your Leadership - Realize Your Full Potential

Q-5: Mark, Is there a specialized training program for leadership?

"Leadership training is a great way to develop your potential and really make the most of your talents. Effective leadership is essential in any organization and is highly sought after by employers. With open learning, you can gain these valuable skills without having to disrupt your current lifestyle.

I have been fascinated over the years by the debate, research and discussion about leadership and management. Increasingly there seems to be a focus on the differences between leadership and management and it seems to me that this has developed in part because of deficits in one or the other.

Most of us would like to become, or to think of ourselves as, strong leaders. There is something appealing about the idea of creating and pursuing a vision and influencing others to support the necessary transitions. True enough, if it was not for good leadership, nothing would change or improve.

Leadership training helps you unlock your full potential and realize your ambitions in the business world. Leadership is firmly at the core of every successful organization, and the effective management of people is a hugely valuable skill that is always in demand.

Open learning allows you to gain leadership training without the disruption of traditional study. With open learning, you can study in your own time and at your own pace, moving through the training course at whatever rate suits you best. This means that you can easily fit your course around your current life commitments, whether you have family responsibilities, a full-time job or any other constraints on your time. You could even earn a prestigious business degree through open learning, and open up a completely new range of career opportunities for yourself!

However, not as many people seem to be as drawn toward being a good manager. Maybe I am misreading the "climate", but management is often associated with the mundane, the routine and a whole range of "left-brain" activity for which the kudos are few.

There appears to be a perception that one can be a leader or a manager, but not much acknowledgement that those skill sets can reside in the same individual. I believe this is an erroneous view.

Leadership:
From Ability to Credibility

My view of leadership and management is that they do require different skill sets, but must co-exist in order for any change to occur effectively. It is like a hand and a glove. Put together they make a great partnership.

Team Building: Developing a Team to Rely On

Q-6: Mark, How can someone build an effective team?

"Team building is very important when it comes to managing people. People are simply more willing to work together, when the atmosphere encourages it. For many organizations, this is quite necessary for the business to run well. When everyone gets along, things just go better. They provide better service to the customer. They work together to deliver satisfaction with smiles. They also help to promote employee retention. Customers are happy, employees are happy, and the world I...

Article Body:

Team building is very important when it comes to managing people. People are simply more willing to work together, when the atmosphere encourages it. For many organizations, this is quite necessary for the business to run well. When everyone gets along, things just go better. They provide better service to the customer. They work together to deliver satisfaction with smiles. They also help to promote employee retention. Customers are happy, employees are happy, and the world is now a better place, right?

Team building is anything but simple. It is not something that can be done overnight. Nor is it something you can force people to do. So, how can you effectively build your team to encourage them to bond and develop working relationships that are positive? There are many things that you can do. Here are some ideas:

• Set the example yourself. As the leader of the team, it is up to you to provide a good relationship with your team players. You want them to feel comfortable with you as well as with others. Do not favor some and do not become too friendly either.

• You can encourage relationships to work by fostering a teamwork style. Make sure that the goals are established and that each team player is aware of them. They should know that you want a teamwork environment that is what you are looking for in your employees.

• Also, provide them with opportunities to get to know each other. Take the team out to dinner on you. Encourage them to talk about their families and lives so that they can bond.

When team building is successful, there are many things that can happen. Not only will the business run better, but you can foster good qualities in individuals to come out. You can have a bond of trust and reliance with your team. Team building is

Leadership:
From Ability to Credibility

an exceptional quality that you should encourage in some form or another with your team."

Leadership Learning: The Real Costs of Not Doing Leadership Training

Q-7: Mark, How can we insure effective leadership?

"A report from the Said Business School at Oxford University in the UK found that British businesses and public sector organizations are wasting almost $140 million on executive education programs that are poorly conceived and delivered.

The study went on to say that 35 per cent of HR directors and 21 per cent of other executives believed that their current training and development programs were meeting corporate strategic objectives. The bulk of the money was being spent o...

A report from the Said Business School at Oxford University in the UK found that British businesses and public sector organizations are wasting almost $140 million on executive education programs that are poorly conceived and delivered.

The study went on to say that 35 per cent of HR directors and 21 per cent of other executives believed that their current training and development programs were meeting corporate strategic objectives. The bulk of the money was being spent on individually developed courses for senior executives.

If those businesses want to quit wasting all that money on bad management training, I know where they can get their money's worth. In addition, it does not have anything to do with having more academics design special courses, events, and outings for senior staff.

Here is a novel idea folks. Why not spend your money on leadership training and development down in the trenches, where it will really do some good?

Most companies do not do nearly enough of that. In 2003, just 7 percent of training budgets in the US were spent on first line leaders and most of that was for learning administration and for prophylactic HR.

The fact is that front line leaders do not get much training at all and precious little of it is actually about leadership skills. Maybe that is because companies think they are saving money by not investing in front line leader training.

True, there is no budget line item absorbing funds that might be spent on the executive dining room, or art for the CEO's office. Nevertheless, there are what economists call "opportunity costs," the costs of not training front line leaders.

There is the opportunity cost of lost productivity.

Leadership:
From Ability to Credibility

Good frontline leadership builds both morale and profitability.

There is the opportunity cost of lost leadership. Great companies develop most of their own leaders. If you have to go outside for leadership, you incur recruitment costs and transition costs.

Finally, there is the cost of lawsuits. Good frontline leadership creates organizations where lawsuits are less likely. In addition, if the company is sued over a supervision issue, defense will be easier if the leaders have been doing their jobs.

How about your company? Do you develop your own leaders? Do you help them develop the skills they need to improve morale and productivity and avoid lawsuits? Think about that the next time you consider the training budget.'

Leadership "True North"

Q-8: Mark, What are true leadership qualities?

"Although some people treat the terms management and leadership as synonyms, the two should be distinguished. As a matter of fact, there can be leaders of completely unorganized groups. On the other hand, there can be managers, as conceived here, only where organized structures create roles.

Although some people treat the terms management

and leadership as synonyms, the two should be distinguished. As a matter of fact, there can be leaders of completely unorganized groups. On the other hand, there can be managers, as conceived here, only where organized structures create roles.

Separating leadership from management has important analytical advantages. It permits leadership to be singled out for study without the encumbrance of qualifications relating to the more general issues of management.

To clarify, leadership is certainly an important aspect of managing. The ability to lead effectively is one of the keys to being an effective manager; also, undertaking the other essentials of managing -- doing the entire managerial job -- has an important bearing on ensuring that a manager will be an effective leader. Managers must exercise all the functions of their role in order to combine human and material resources to achieve objectives. The key to doing this is the existence of a clear role and a degree of discretion or authority to support the manager's actions.

The essence of leadership is followership. In other words, it is the willingness of other people to follow that makes a person a leader. Moreover, people tend to follow those whom they see as providing a means of achieving their own desires, wants and needs. Leadership and motivation are closely interconnected. By understanding motivation, one can appreciate better, what people want and why

Leadership:
From Ability to Credibility

they act as they do. In addition, leaders may not only respond to subordinates' motivations but also arouse or dampen them by means of the organizational climate they develop. Both these factors are as important to leadership as they are to management.

Leadership can be defined as influence, that is, the art of influencing people so that they will strive willingly and enthusiastically toward the achievement of group goals. Ideally, people should be encouraged to develop not only a willingness to work but also a willingness to work with zeal and confidence.

Leadership: Is It For You?

Q-9: Mark, Is leadership for everyone?

"Leadership is something that is fundamentally part of a society. It is necessary in any good society that someone stands up and takes charge. Leadership is essential, we know that, but does that mean everyone out there is a leader? The fact of the matter is that some individuals are not made to be leaders. They are followers. In addition, just as important in society as leaders are followers. So, where do you lie? Are you going to play leadership roles within your life?

Leadership is something that is fundamentally part of a society. It is necessary in any good society that someone stands up and takes charge. Leadership is essential, we know that, but does that mean everyone out there is a leader? The fact of the matter is that some individuals are not made to be leaders. They are followers. In addition, just as important in society as leaders are followers. So, where do you lie? Are you going to play leadership roles within your life?

For many people, the instincts to take those leadership roles just come to them. It is just something that happens. They step up to the plate when needed. They respond first in class. They take charge of the baseball game on the playground. They step up to the plate on the job. While you cannot be first in every case, individual that have leadership skills will often be seen and heard throughout their lives.

However, not all leaders are born with this talent. Many of them must learn it. People with an ambition to be a leader can do so by taking classes and studying the necessary skills that it takes to be a leader. While all of this may sound simple, it can be quite a task to learn. It is hard to teach a person to react in a situation that is not planned well.

Because leaders are determined by their actions, we often see that leadership roles are filled with individuals who put themselves out there to be chosen, so to speak. However, this is not always the case. In many cases of emergency, leaders are those that take charge long before anyone else reacts. In that, these individuals will have a cool

Leadership:
From Ability to Credibility

head about themselves and be able to see the necessary work ahead while others are worrying, panicking or simply in shock. These are probably the true leaders in our society."

Leadership: Is Mentoring For You?

Q-10: Mark, Can leadership be taught by anyone?

"If you are considering mentoring a younger person, here are some things to think about. Make sure that mentoring is for you. Most effective mentors truly, deeply enjoy helping younger people grow and develop. Make sure you are likely to enjoy the process before you take it on.

Make sure you have the time and flexibility. If your schedule is already overloaded or you're under stress at home, you might want to consider holding off on a mentoring commitment until you are sure of your commitment."

If you are considering mentoring a younger person, here are some things to think about. Make sure that mentoring is for you. Most effective mentors truly, deeply enjoy helping younger people grow and develop. Make sure you are likely to enjoy the process before you take it on.

Make sure you have the time and flexibility. If your schedule is already overloaded or you are under stress at home, you might want to consider holding off on a mentoring commitment until things are a little less hectic.

Make sure you know what you bring to the table. None of us is good at everything, but every one of us is really good at something. If you know, what you are good at and what other things you may bring to the table, you are more likely to be successful.

In his excellent book, Winning, Jack Welch says that "There is no one right mentor. There are many right mentors." From your perspective, that means you do not have to do everything. You are not the only place that your protégé should get help.

Make sure you know what kind of people you like to work with and which ones are hard for you. Mentoring should be a pleasant relationship for both of you.

Make sure you know what you expect from your protégé. It is a good idea to tell him or her you expect them to do. Clear expectations are vital to a mentoring relationship.

Make sure you know that a good mentoring relationship should be a good experience for both of you. You should both enjoy it. You should both grow and develop. Moreover, you should both make a friend for life.

Mentoring can be one of the most rewarding experiences of your career or it can be a frustrating

Leadership:
From Ability to Credibility

and time-consuming trial. Make sure you know what you're getting into."

Leadership Is Action... Not Position

Q-11: Mark, What are the leadership qualities that separate true leaders from the rest of us?

"People respond to good leadership! Period! It is in all aspects of our lives, not just business. A mother is a leader in her home; a son may be leader of a team sport or a daughter the leader of the debate team. A group relies on the person in charge to actually lead them to success. A true leader is highly ethical, honest and respected.

In our society, we have leaders and followers. Are we born to one or the other? No! Can you hone your leadership skills? Absolutely!

People respond to good leadership! Period! It is in all aspects of our lives, not just business. A mother is a leader in her home; a son may be leader of a team sport or a daughter the leader of the debate team. A group relies on the person in charge to actually lead them to success. A true leader is highly ethical, honest and respected.

In our society, we have leaders and followers. Are we born to one or the other? No! Can you hone your leadership skills? Absolutely!

The leaders that I admire seem to have all of these in place:

a) They think BIG! They do not put a ceiling in place. Instead, no limit is set as to how big or how much better something can be.

b) The goals are firmly set in place and the eye does not come off it.

c) They make known to all involved the final product that they are all going for, example, if you sell widgets, it takes x number of widgets to be affluent, or you want to win that football game and ultimately the title. Know what you are going for.

d) They can get compliance to orders.

e) When goals are met they set new goals or raise the bar.

People will follow your lead willingly if you are honest, ethical, if you are consistent and treat them with respect. Rewarding someone when a job is well done is always appreciated. A good leader will also off load someone who consistently hinders the group who is just not a team player.

You can improve your own self- respect and become an inspiration to others. How great is that!"

How One-on-One Executive Coaching Can Work For You

Q-12: Mark, Can anyone be an executive coach?

"One-on-One executive coaching can give your leaders the creativity and training they need to

Leadership:
From Ability to Credibility

make your organization excel. Read more to see how.

Does your company need a jumpstart? Are revenue low, morale declining, and your leadership tactics no longer making an impact? This may be the perfect time to look into leadership coaching.

A good executive coaching program should do more than just set you up with a speaker reading over a PowerPoint presentation. Team up your senior leaders with a good corporate coaching program, and you could be discussing fostering relationships, building strategy, and improving revenue and communications all while hitting the slopes, climbing a mountain or rafting some white water. It is easy to connect in an environment where you can be creative, and think outside the box.

A good leadership system can make all the difference in your organization. It effects; communication, human performance, accountability, delivery and measurement. A one-on-one approach, and a program that is tailored to suit your organization's specific needs, is the best choice in executive coaching.

There are a few important things to consider if you want to engage in an executive coaching program. Look for a company that will provide you with someone who is more than just a speaker. You want to be paired up with someone who will be a trusted advisor to you as your organization grows and changes. In addition, a good coaching program will include industry consultants to provide expert advice in some technical areas. Talk to your consultant about the specific goals you want your leadership program to meet. Every business or organization needs direction in a different area or department. This is what makes a one-on-one coaching program so unique; you work on meeting goals where your company needs it the most."

The foundation of coaching is rooted in the possibility for advancement, progress, achievement and success. The reasoning to develop effective coaching methods will foster improvement to existing conditions and advancement in future endeavors. The most productive methods to effective coaching involve relationship building. The interaction between people is the key factor in coaching is success. Once the extent of a coach's involvement is determined, the scope of interaction and direction can be tailored to achieve the maximum benefit. The key factor in this enterprise is people engagement. The physical, psychological and emotional engagement combined with trust and empathy for hierarchy, position, status, intent and focus are all related in a coach's tool kit.
The coaching relationship is founded on mutual trust and respect. The tie that binds interaction is effective communication between stakeholders. An organization's culture and expression of intended results drives the coach's focus. How well developed the coach's abilities are a clear reflection

Leadership:
From Ability to Credibility

of how effective the relationships are between coach and mentees. The results are dynamic and persuasive.

Your Call to Action

Ignorance on Fire Beats Knowledge on Ice!

There are two important differences between motivation and inspiration. It will become important to learn what they are to lead you to success. I will teach you to understand why:

- You are the Master of Your Success.
- You are the Master of Your
- Achievements.

You are the Master of Wealth, Freedom and Happiness.

I believe that there are only three types of people:

1. The type of person that watches things happens.

2. The type of person that makes things happens.

3. The type of person that asks, "What happened?"

<u>Which are you?</u>

Mark Zupo

I teach you how to dispel the myths of failure, lack of control, and negative influences of other people. I will teach you how to find your "Real Dream System" to empower you with the strength and desire to "Be All You Can Be" and "All You Want to be!" If it has been done before, then you can do it too! Be The First To Imagine It, And then...Achieve What You Can Believe!

Here, you will learn three simple goal-setting methods that you can do before you are done brushing your teeth in the morning. You will learn how you can visualize your dreams and make them a reality. You will learn how you can do anything, be anything and achieve anything that anyone else can do, be and achieve.

"Oh, really?" you say. Yes really! If it has been done before, someone just like you did it. So what makes you think that you cannot do it? They had money, they had time, they had help, they had....who cares what they had? You have the same resources within your reach and...all you have to do is ask.

When it comes to life and business, it is no coincidence that some people always seem to fail while others always seem to flourish. For sure, chance plays a role in everything. Nevertheless, as

Leadership:
From Ability to Credibility

individuals, as business-owners, as thinkers and as parents, we have a significant degree of control over our lives.

Now, we can use the control that we have to influence outcomes negatively. Alternatively, we can use it to influence outcomes in our favor and in the favor of those, we care about most. When we use our control poorly or when we do not use it at all, it should come as no surprise that our outcomes are bad. In addition, when we use our control thoughtfully and carefully, it should be less surprising when we succeed.

Let me give you an example. At work, your employer considers you for a promotion; however, at the same time, she considers several of your co-workers for the same promotion. Now, as many do, you might immediately say, "There's nothing I can do to influence my boss in my favor. Instead, this decision will be determined by things that are out of my control." Moreover, of course, when the day comes, you will not get that promotion. Instead, someone who pushed hard to demonstrate his worthiness for the position will get the job. You will be left wondering why that person is always successful and always gets promotions, raises, and the adoration of management.

You might even feel resentment toward that person, even though you consider him a friend. When it comes down to it, though, it was not your friend who caused you to miss the promotion (or at least not to give yourself the best shot at getting it). Rather, it was your own behavior that prevented your boss from seriously considering you as a candidate.

Fortunately, for you, this book is all about situations just like the one we described above. It is about feeling powerless when you are not, experiencing bad outcomes when there is no reason to and, finally, about making sure this problem stops.

"A diamond in an ugly setting... is still a diamond."

Mark Zupo - 2008

Most importantly, this book is about success. It is about extracting the characteristics of others that make them successful at work, in parenthood or in the workplace, and then adopting those

Leadership:
From Ability to Credibility

characteristics for your own use.

So, without further ado, let us take the plunge. Today, you will stop telling yourself that you have no control over your life; and today, you will learn exactly what it means to take that control, grasp it firmly and use it to achieve success in all areas of your life. Set a goal, make a plan and DO IT!

"The greatest manifestation of productive effort is celebrated...at the Bank!"

- **Unknown**

Mentorship Programs: Follow the Leader

Learn from a model of success

You need to mentor others to change, create, empower, lead, build, enable, direct and guide others' lives to their specific independence and triumphs.

Mentoring versus Coaching

Definition: Mentor – *noun*

1. A wise and trusted counselor or teacher.

An influential senior sponsor or supporter.

2. Definition: Coach – *verb/noun*

To give instruction or advice in the capacity of a coach. A person who gives instruction.

What is a Mentor?

When we think of other people who helped us in our lives because of their experience and expertise or because of their interest or consideration towards us, we think of them as nice people who gave of themselves. We think of them as being kind to us or as helping, we reach our goals or expectations. Whenever we were faced with a challenge or problem that seemed too hard for us to fix, those people used their life experiences as guidance to help us. This could have been as a child, in school, at home or even at work. Usually they were keen to point out talents that we did not know we had or that we had not yet used.

Mentors come in many forms. They are teachers, parents, coworkers, bosses, other students, friends and relatives. In the past, people were mentored personally and in someone else's presence; but today's technology allows for mentoring to take place via many electronic means, and it eliminates the

Leadership:
From Ability to Credibility

challenges presented by time and distance. The ability to mentor many people at one time via an electronic method is an invaluable tool and actually provides for many more opportunities for the participants. It helps to bring together people from many occupations and cultural backgrounds.

As a mentor, you will deliver the following:

- **Information**

  ✓ A Mentor will share his life and business experience and knowledge.

- **Methodolog**y

  ✓ A Mentor will deliver a precise and formatted methodology as a template for success.

- **Instruction**

  ✓ A Mentor will direct the mentees with pre-programmed direction and focus.

- **Opportunity**

- ✓ A Mentor will guide the mentee in various forms of opportunity with industry knowledge and experience.

- **Challenges**

- ✓ A Mentor will challenge and stimulate curiosity while building confidence and trust.

- **Support**

- ✓ A Mentor will build trust and achievement through his support.

- **Guidance**

- ✓ A Mentor will use his or her experience to guide the mentee in a focused and direct course to achieve the best outcome.

- **Goals and Expectations**

- ✓ A Mentor will give guidance and help to open lines of communication while defining a mentee's goals and objectives.

- **Advice**

- ✓ A Mentor will guide and help a mentee in reaching goals.

Leadership:
From Ability to Credibility

- **Models of Success**

✓ A Mentor will change, create, share, empower, lead, build, enable, direct and guide the lives of his mentees to their specific independence and triumphs.

Mentor Program Guidelines

A mentorship program offers a mentee the unique opportunity to develop a relationship with a mentor who is more experienced and skilled in the area that he wants to learn about. A mentor's experiences, perspectives and general wisdom can be effective tools for his mentee's success. Although a mentor and his mentee may talk frequently, the process begins with a delivery of valuable information or insight into the program.

For the program to work well and be a rewarding experience, there are some guidelines that must be met:

- Mentees should be able to rely on their mentors to keep them informed and up-to-date with all important information.

Mark Zupo

- A mentor should help a mentee develop a plan of action and set goals for success.

- Student-mentees should share their needs and wants and talk to their mentors about what they hope to gain from the program.

- A mentor program is a dynamic system to teach processes, and it requires mutual cooperation between both parties.

- Mentees should be willing to share effective feedback to their mentors, helping them to provide good content.

- A mentor is responsible for developing the mentee's fullest potential and strengths and for eliminating weaknesses that inhibit growth and success.

"Think like a winner and act like a champion,
In other words, fake it till you make it!"
Mark Zupo -2009

It should be considered that although you might coach other people in the improvement of their lives, it is even more important that you build trust between you and your mentees.

I charge more than $1,000 per hour with

Leadership:
From Ability to Credibility

a 3-hour minimum for authoritative mentoring. Mentoring people is one of the most lucrative revenue streams that you will ever find. The process to develop a mentor program is one that can be done anywhere in the world, at any time of the day or week.

-Systemization

The model for mentoring is to mentor many people at one time; although you are selling your knowledge at a cheaper rate because you have delivered the same information to more people at one time as opposed to a few people at one time.

As a mentor, you guide your mentees in the safest and most productive methods or paths that they should take. A clear example of a "mentor" program in the professional world is a franchise. There are many like McDonald's, drug stores, car washes and movie theaters. You can surely understand that a franchise is designed for the franchisees to be as productive and profitable as humanly possible. If the individual storeowners succeed and make money, then the company that holds the franchise makes money and everyone is happy.

-Standardization

A huge benefit of a mentorship program is to set up your program so mentees are challenged to perform and to measure their performance. Without measurement and goals, mentees will falter und usually fail, even with your guidance? One of the challenges for someone who owns a franchisee is that he or she cannot alter or wander from the absolute prescribed method, product or practice of the franchise.

-Automation

Contact with your mentees is an absolute must. Usually you will give them a private method to contact you with questions or problems. Email is one of the best methods to remain in contact to fully understand what the issue is so that the correct response is sent.

-Delegation

A comprehensive program is the best model for your success, as well as for the mentees' success. Pure and concise content, with an all-inclusive program, is the key to making a successful mentor program.

Delegation exists when the mentees have a support partner whose interest in their

Leadership:
From Ability to Credibility

success is founded on mutual benefit. Once mentees are dedicated to their own success and commit to following your instructions, they will require a complete and comprehensive program to follow.

When you mentor more than one mentee, there is a synergy between mentees and mentor that will have a dynamic life of its own that will benefit everyone who participates.

"If you think you can or you think you can't... Either way you're right!"

- **Henry Ford**

7-Level Success Mentorship Program™

Copy Success

-Get a Mentor, Get a Mentor, and Get a Mentor!

One method that I use to coach people who are reluctant to follow through with an assignment is to require them to sign a check made out for $100 to someone they do not like. Then the check is given to a loyal friend who wants to see them succeed and is sworn to send the check if they fail to perform. The key word here is DO NOT like. The thought of giving away your money to someone you do not like is usually a motivator to achievement.

"To find success, you have to begin looking in the right direction, to get to the place where your success lives; you have to start where you stand."

- **Mark Zupo**

A note from Mark

First, I would like to say thank you for your trust.

I know there is a world of options out there but you chose to read my book. That is a very humbling and special thing for me. As a thought-leader and business mentor, I have worked with businesses and people all over the world. I have worked with educators, business owners, individuals, entrepreneurs, lawyers, consultants, coaches, trainers and more. As founder of the ***7-Level Success Academy*®** I have helped these same people achieve personal and business success, improvement to life and happiness. Maybe I can help you too.

As an entrepreneur for more than 35 years, I believe that my success comes from an absolute lust for learning and from working harder helping other people more than helping myself. I will always be a student in one form or another. In fact, I prefer that I am a leader by choice and design rather than by accidental need.

> **"The choice to lead is a choice to serve"**
> **- Mark Zupo**

Mark's top-selling books!:

1. **"You Deserve to be Rich"**
   The Secrets to Earning What You're Really Worth

2. **From Mess to Millionaire**
   One Man's Story of Failure to Success

3. **Money Mouth - Speak for Yourself**
   The 7-Secrets of How to Make your Living Speaking

4. **Mind Your Business!**
   The Ultimate Guide to Repurpose Your Life Experience, Passions, Education and Knowledge

5. **100 Quotes I live by**
   Words of wisdom and Insight

6. **Achieve What You Can Believe**
   Finding success in self-empowerment

Leadership:
From Ability to Credibility

Appendix One

Sources and Resources

Mark's speaking career in industry spans 25 years. He has delivered more-than, 1,200 presentations. He has authored and co-authored many books on self-development, business development techniques and marketing enterprises. Mark speaks on several topics that enlighten, entertain and motivate his audiences to action!

Mark's most requested Topics/Programs:
- **My Adversity University**

 "Build Power, Credibility and Respect from Life's Lessons"
- **Champion Your Success**

"Achieve What You Believe, Believe What You Can Achieve'
- **7-Secrets of Business Success**

"The Keys to Wealth and Freedom"
- **Leadership**

"From Ability to Credibility"

Schedule Mark to Speak at Your Next Event!
Contact us: 1-678-640-0585
09:00 – 5:00 EST
On-line:
www.MarkZupo.com
markzupo@gmail.com

Mark Zupo

Key Questions That Set You Apart

Am I a sponge for discovery and opportunity?
Do I devour information that keeps me sharp to the current events that affect my markets?
Am I a true optimist?
Do I think of problems as opportunities?
Am I forward-looking?
Am I satisfied with the status quo?
Am I a risk-taker?
Do I usually act on my hunches?
Do I have passion?
Do I stick to my efforts instead of quitting? Do I love what I do?
Am I competitive?
Do I think in competitive terms to motivate me?
Am I money wise?
Do I understand costs and values?
Am I time conscious?
Do I know the value of time and how to use it?
Am I overtly curious?
Do I ask many questions about how things work?
Am I a solitary worker?
Do I work best by myself or on a team?
Am I professional at all times?
Am I easily distracted by outside influences?
Do I have high energy?
Do I maintain myself, my well-being and my mental stability?

Leadership:
From Ability to Credibility

7-Level Success Seminars™
Mind Your Business Seminars™
Mark Zupo Seminars™

...Reserve your seat NOW!

"MAKE YOUR BUSINESS YOUR LIFE AND MAKE YOUR LIFE YOUR BUSINESS!"

- MARK ZUPO

Leadership:
From Ability to Credibility

ABOUT THE AUTHOR

Mark Zupo is an "Accomplished Entrepreneur" who has devoted his life to helping others succeed in their goals and dreams. His goal is to help you fulfill your career goals and achieve financial freedom and independence by building the successful..."Business of You!" Mark's consulting and e-Business acumen remains unequaled as a *Life-Success Authority*. Mark is a leader, entrepreneur and mentor to many.

Mark Zupo is a dynamic and insightful speaker, recognized for his empowering and motivational focus to your success. As a driven leader with a commanding presence, he motivates, inspires, energizes and empowers his audience.

Mark Zupo has been the driving force in changing the lives of anyone within range of his voice. Mark's "3-Foot Rule" makes him one of the most sought-after speakers in his industry.

Mark's speaking career in industry spans 25 years and he has delivered more-than, 1,200 presentations. From his experiences he has authored and co-authored many books on self-development, business development techniques and marketing enterprises. Find the topic or topics that are a sure fit for you and your organization, and schedule Mark to speak at your event soon.

Mark Zupo

"The toughest lessons learned are the best lessons earned"

- **Mark Zupo**

www.7LevelSuccess.com

www.MarkZupo.com

Leadership:
From Ability to Credibility

References

Balkundi, P., Kilduff, M., & Harrison, D. A. (2011, November). Centrality and charisma: Comparing how leader networks and attributions affect team performance. *Journal of Applied Psychology* 96 (6), 1209-1222

Bell, A. H., & Smith, D. M. (2010). *Developing leadership abilities* (2nd ed.). Upper Saddle River, NJ: Prentice Hall.

Bono, J., & Judge, T. (2004). Personality and transformational and transactional leadership: A meta-analysis. *Journal of Applied Psychology,* 89, 901-910.

Deal, T., & Peterson, K. D. (2009). *Shaping school culture: Pitfalls, paradoxes and promises* (2nd ed.). San Francisco, CA: Jossey-Bass.

George, B., & Sims, P. (2007). *True North: Discover your authentic leadership.* San Francisco, CA Wiley. ISBN: 978-0787987510

Kouzes, J. M., & Posner, B. Z. (2007). *The Leadership Challenge*. San Francisco, CA: Jossey-Bass.

Kouzes, J., & Posner, B. (2008). *The leadership challenge.* 4th ed. San Francisco, CA Jossey-Bass. ISBN: 9780787984915

Leithwood, K. A. The move toward transformational leadership. Educational Leadership vol. 49 no. (5)(1992). pp. 8–12.

Northouse, P. G. (2007). *Leadership: Theory and practice.* (5th ed.). Thousand Oaks, CA: Sage.

Palmer, B., Walls, M., Burgess, Z., & Stough, C. (2001). Emotional intelligence and effective leadership. *Leadership and Organization Development Journal, 22,* 5-10.

Reeves, D. B. (2004). *Accountability in action: A blueprint for learning organizations* (2nd ed.). Englewood, CO: Advanced Learning Press.

Slaski, M. and Cartwright, S. (2003), Emotional intelligence training and its implications for stress, health and performance. Stress and Health, 19: 233–239. doi: 10.1002/smi.979

Wasylyshn, K., Shorey, H., & Chaffin, J. (2012, December). Patterns of leadership behavior: Implications for successful executive coaching outcomes. *Coaching Psychologist, 8*(2), 74-85.

Watkin, C. (2000), Developing Emotional Intelligence. International Journal of Selection and Assessment, 8: 89–92. doi: 10.1111/1468-2389.00137

Whitman, Daniel S., "Emotional Intelligence and Leadership in Organization: A Meta-analytic Test of Process Mechanisms" (2009). *FIU Electronic Theses and Dissertations.* Paper113. Retrieved from: http://digitalcommons.fiu.edu/etd/113

Leadership:
From Ability to Credibility

DISCLAIMER

...just to keep the lawyers happy.

This information is not presented by a medical practitioner and is for educational and informational purposes only. The content is not intended to be a substitute for professional medical advice, diagnosis, or treatment. Always seek the advice of your physician or other qualified health care provider with any questions you may have regarding a medical condition. Never disregard professional medical advice or delay in seeking it because of something you have read or heard.

This information in this book is strictly for informational and educational purposes only. The author and/or publisher do not guarantee that anyone using any of the information, tips, techniques, etc. from this book will become successful. The author and/or publisher shall have neither liability nor responsibility to anyone with respect to any loss or damage caused, or alleged to be caused, directly or indirectly by the information contained in this book. No guarantees are made that you will achieve any results from our ideas and techniques in our material. The information presented herein represents the view of the author as of the date of publication. The author reserves the right to alter and update his opinion Any slights of people or organizations are unintentional. You should be aware of any laws which govern business transactions or other business practices in your country and state. Any reference to any person or business whether living or dead is purely coincidental. We do not purport this as a "get rich scheme." All trademarks belong to their respective owners.

The publisher has strived to be as accurate and complete as possible in the creation of this report, notwithstanding the fact that he does not warrant or represent at any time that the contents within are accurate, due to the rapidly changing nature of the business. However, there may be mistakes in typography or content. The purpose of this e-book is to educate.

While all attempts have been made to verify information provided in this publication, the publisher assumes no responsibility for errors, omissions, or contrary interpretation of the subject matter herein. Any perceived slights of specific persons, peoples, or organizations are unintentional.

This book is a common-sense guide to self-improvement. In practical advice books, like in anything else in life, there are no guarantees of income made. Readers are cautioned to reply with their own judgment about their individual

Leadership:
From Ability to Credibility

circumstances and to act accordingly. This book is not intended for use as a source of legal, business, accounting or financial advice. All readers are advised to seek services of competent professionals in legal, business, accounting and finance fields.

This information is presented for educational and informational purposes only and is not intended to be a substitute for professional advice. Never disregard professional advice or delay in seeking it because of something read or heard.

We make every effort to ensure that we accurately represent our products and services and their potential for income. Earning and income statements made by our company and its customers are estimates of what we think you can possibly earn based on your individual effort, skill, experience and effort only.. There is no guarantee that you will make the level of income you desire, and you accept the risk that the earnings and income statements differ by individual.

As with any business, your results may vary and will be based on your individual capacity, business experience, expertise, and level of desire. The testimonials and examples used are exceptional results, which do not apply to the average purchaser, and are not intended to represent or guarantee that anyone will achieve the same or similar results. Each individual's success depends on his or her background, dedication, desire and motivation.

The use of our information, products and services should be based on your own due diligence, and you hold harmless our company for any success or failure of your business that is directly or indirectly related to the purchase and use of our information, products and services.

There are no guarantees concerning the level of success you may experience. The testimonials and examples used are exceptional results, which do not apply to the average purchaser, and are not intended to represent or guarantee that anyone will achieve the same or similar results. Each individual's success depends on his or her background, dedication, desire and motivation.

There is no assurance that examples of past earnings can be duplicated and we cannot guarantee your future results and/or success. There are unknown risks in business and on the internet and in practical application in life and business that we cannot foresee which can reduce results. We are not responsible for your actions.

Leadership:
From Ability to Credibility

The use of our information, products and services should be based on your own due diligence and you hold harmless our company for any success or failure of your business that is directly or indirectly related to the purchase and use of our information, products and services.

Mark Zupo

Leadership:
From Ability to Credibility

Mark Zupo